Woman: Survivor in the Church

Woman: Survivor in the Church

by

Joan Ohanneson

HARPER & ROW, PUBLISHERS, New York
Cambridge, Philadelphia, San Francisco, Washington,
London, Mexico City, São Paulo, Singapore, Sydney

Cover and book design: Maria Mazzara

Library of Congress Catalog Card Number: 79-56865
ISBN: 0-86683-607-1 (previously ISBN: 0-03-056671-1)

Printed in the United States of America.

5   4   3

Acknowledgments

*F*IRST, TO ALL THE WOMEN, many of them strangers, who trusted me with their stories by reaching deep into their lives to share their needs, dreams, prayers, and pain. I can only be reverent toward the request of some for anonymity.

Secondly, to all the women who taught me by their witness, wisdom, scholarship, and poetry. The seeds they planted in my head and heart have come to harvest in this book.

Thanks are due to Robert Belvin of the San Jose Public Library and to Rev. John F. Mattingly, S.S. and Pam Nurse of St. Patrick's Seminary Library, Menlo Park, Cal.; to Rev. William T. O'Keeffe, S.S., for important information regarding ministry to Catholics who are separated and divorced; to Rev. John Carville for kind assistance with referrals; and for the affirmation of so many people at Winston Press, particularly John Welshons, Dee Ready, and especially my editor, Pat Lassonde, whose sensitivity and professionalism were special gifts. I am also personally grateful to my typist, Betty Van Arsdale, whose genuine interest and generosity of spirit were continuing sources of support.

I am deeply indebted to many, many special friends who "prayed me through," especially Eileen Cahill, Mary Beth Onk, Verna Jarboe, Irene Ohanessian, and Patricia Helin.

But I can find no words for the most life-giving gift of all— the invaluable input and abiding love of my daughters, Kim, Beth, Jill, and Erin, and the unfailing, deeply sustaining daily encouragement of my husband, Greg. I can only hope that they know in their hearts that this book was born because they believed in me.

Joan Ohanneson
San Jose, California

Foreword

*A*S I REFLECT UPON THE
struggles of women for justice and for the truth about their
position in the world and in the Church today, I recall a passage
in a letter of Teilhard de Chardin to his cousin Marguerite on
December 13, 1918, from the front, at the close of World War I:*

> You can't imagine what intensity of desire I sometimes feel
> in this connexion, [sic] and what impotence! What keeps
> me calm is my complete confidence that if there is a ray of
> light in "my gospel," somehow or other the ray will shine
> forth. At the worst—of this I'm sure—it will reappear in
> another heart,—all the richer, I hope, for having been faith-
> fully guarded in me.

Joan Ohanneson makes a significant contribution to the
effort of making that "ray of light" visible in *Woman: Survivor in
the Church*. The descriptions she gives of woman's pains, struggles, and survival are etched with actual experiences of women
of courage, hope, and creativity. She makes one sense the
strength and self-determination of today's women as they forge
ahead into an area that is without footpaths, landmarks, clear-
ings, into environs swept away by the tidal wave of history. Their
legacy is one of anonymity bereft of genuine woman-models.

Woman: Survivor in the Church is addressed to women, first
of all, but equally to men. Churchwomen—the religious, the
married, and especially the single—are challenged to dialogue
with other women, with the clergy, with men within the Church.
The author examines the present inadequacies of that dialogue
and urges both men and women to respond to the hopes

expressed in documents of Vatican II and to the thoughts of some of the bishops of the United States who have responded to the issue of women in the Church.

The wholeness of her approach as well as the lack of expressed bitterness in it makes me, and I hope all of her readers, confident that we shall achieve the goal to "live in God fully in our womanhood."**

Sister Mary Anthony Wagner, OSB
St. Benedict's Convent
St. Joseph, Minnesota

---

*Teilhard de Chardin, *The Making of a Mind*, transl. René Hague (New York: Harper and Row, 1965), p. 269.
**Joan Ohanneson, *Woman: Survivor in the Church* (Minneapolis: Winston Press, 1980), p. 32.

Contents

To
my mother
Lee Delmonico
whose legacies
of
faith and love
taught me
to
survive

Introduction

ONCE UPON A TIME THERE
was a traveling woman who set out to find her fortune in
freckles.

One day as she walked along, she saw a small girl playing by
a bridge. When the child looked up at her, hope rose like a
meadowlark in the weary woman's heart.

"Oh, little girl," said the woman, "I have wandered over half
the earth looking for someone to give me some freckles. You
have so many...Please!....Won't you give some to me?"

The little girl laughed. "Are they really so wonderful?" she
asked her.

"Oh, yes!" said the woman. "Oh, yes indeed!"

"Then they are yours," said the child. "And though I will
wear them for you as a kindness, from this moment on, they
belong to you!"

The weary woman's eyes filled with tears. "How can I thank
you?" she said. "What can I give you in return?"

"Give me?" said the child. "But you gave me my freckles!
Without you, I never would have known they were beautiful,"
the little girl said.

No one ever told me...

Finish that sentence with your own words...with your own
life.

No one ever told me I was talented...or organized...or
bright...or funny.

No one ever told me I was *gifted* (in healing, in
reconciliation).

No one ever told me I was *chosen* (out of and for the
community).

No one ever told me I was *called* (to exercise my talents, my uniqueness in ministry).

No one ever told me...so I never knew!

And because I am human, I *need* the words....

I need to *hear* them...from myself, from others...just as I need to *listen*.

No....No one ever told me....

But what is even more important, no one ever *asked* me... even though I comprise over half the membership of the church.

No one ever asked me what *I* thought, how *I* felt, what *I* needed...who *I* dreamed of becoming!

I have been waiting...I have been waiting for centuries... and I have grown weary of *work* without words, without hope, without promises! I am tired of having God used against me in the politics of exclusion, when I am told, at the same time, that I am a pearl of great price.

And so, ...since no one has asked me, I must begin to ask myself and others of my kind. Indeed, it seems that I no longer have a choice. Pope Paul VI reminds me that "Each person is responsible for her self-fulfillment, even as that person is for salvation."[1]

And so, that is what we will be about in this book....Taking that first step in the process of self-fulfillment by defining *who we are*...by speaking *our* words...by sharing *our* meaning...by releasing *our* dreams!

And in doing so...let us feel, for once, that we are the most important people in the world.

Let us love ourselves by trusting our questions...confident that the Holy Spirit has brought us to this moment to encourage us to a sense of our own self-definition, our own potential, our own wholeness.

> For Jesus said to his disciples...to you and to me...
> I do not call you servants any longer,
> because a servant does not know what his master is
>   doing.

Instead, I call you friends
because I have told you everything I have heard
    from my Father.
You did not choose me;
I chose you and appointed you to go and bear much
    fruit,
the kind of fruit that endures.
And so the Father will give you
whatever you ask of him in my name (Jn 15:15-17).

Let us begin in reverence by ministering as women to one
another and to ourselves.

Legacy

her body ripples like a river
    sending signals to the sea.
the shell in her hand
speaks of long-dead secrets
    of promises whispered to a swollen moon.
she holds the wisdom of the sage
who draws fiery signs in the water
and knows the song of the sailor
who has conquered an ocean.
she wields the power of oblivion
with a strong, sure hand—
this woman of dark night and water,
daughter of sorrow and ancient sun.

kim a. ohanneson

CHAPTER ONE

Where Have Women Been?
Hidden Treasure

THEY ARE THERE WAITING, waiting for us to find them—beautiful women, courageous women, women who glowed with brilliance as they witnessed with their brains and their bodies, their strength and their tenderness. They wait like jewels covered over by the sand of silent centuries, like diamonds and sapphires buried deep in deserts, obscured by the fog of anonymity. A few have been saved and stored up in the velvet-lined coffers of history. They were placed, like strands of pearls, around our necks when we were young.

We touched them time and again until the beads took on our skin glow and the pearls became part of us: the Marys—the best, the most beloved Blessed Lady; then the most-mentioned Mary Magdalene; followed, certainly, by the Mary described as Martha's sister (the one who always made us feel uncomfortable, because we never understood her as she sat, never seeing how much needed to be done). We said the Mary names with a kind of reverence, but were these women real to us? Did we care enough about them to ever really want to know them, to somehow seek them out to be our friends?

Our fingers moved along the necklace; the beads grew smaller but were still important: Saint Thérèse, the Little Flower, who canonized the "ordinary" (as children we thought, "Gosh, maybe there's hope for me!"); Bernadette of Lourdes, listed as "visionary," described at fourteen years as "ailing and under-sized, sensitive and of pleasant disposition but accounted backward and slow"[1]; and memorable in my confusing adolescence,

Saint Mary Goretti, the teenager, who chose to lose her life rather than her virginity.

Looking back now, it seems there were others, like the foundresses of religious orders. But they were always shadows behind a screen of pure perfection when Sister spoke of them in class or Sunday school. I never remember that they had names.

Occasionally, the Bible, the Old Testament, lifted up a woman who flashed like a momentary meteor. But when I tried, with excitement, to capture her, to find out more about her, she was gone.

There must have been others, but they eluded me. With some exceptions, there were only fragmentary crumbs of information: "though she is the patron saint of the city and university of Oxford, little can be said for certain about Saint Frideswide."[2] A scanty legacy for twenty centuries, but I never questioned it. The Blessed Mother was, for me, always more than enough.

This is not so for my daughters. "If women have always comprised more than half the church membership, what have they been doing, Mother, where have they been?"

Where indeed?

I wonder how different my self-image as a Christian woman would have been, if the stories of these women had been told to me when I needed them. I needed to know how vital women were to Jesus in his ministry; how he chose to reveal his identity to the Samaritan woman (rather than to the apostles) by telling her of his mission as the Messiah; how he appeared to women first with the news, the reality of his resurrection, the central truth of Christianity.

Surely this was no accident. Jesus did not relate to women in this way purely by chance.

Why, young women ask, wasn't this proclaimed from the pulpits; why wasn't this dignity declared over and over again to women throughout history?

I needed to know about Phoebe, who is remembered for her hospitality and is considered by many to be the first deaconess.[3] "I recommend to you our sister Phoebe, who serves the church at Cenchreae. Receive her in the Lord's name as God's people should, and give her any help she may need from you, for she has been a good friend of many people and also to me" (Ro 16:1-2).

And how the example of Priscilla, that "fellow worker" of Saint Paul's (Ro 16:3), would have affirmed my mother as she stirred the beans at potluck suppers and raised money for the parish school gym! Even though she never got out of the kitchen, either at church or at home, it might have been good for my mother to know that women once were "equal workers with men" in the infant church—that Priscilla was indeed mentioned before her husband in both the Acts of the Apostles and in Romans.

Priscilla was credited with teaching Christian doctrine to Apollos, a highly literate Jew who subsequently was to play a major role in the church in Corinth.[4] (When mothers tried to find the time to spend precious hours teaching catechism in the parish, they might have taken courage from this fact.) When I tried to recruit shy and insecure women to assume roles of leadership in the parish or in the Catholic school system, I wish I could have shared with them the excitement of the women who were leaders of the church in its early history. That church, characterized by the Holy Spirit, called forth and celebrated the gifts and charisms of *each member* of the community, whether male or female.

I think back now to the hundreds of hours I spent in meetings of the altar guild, meetings in which the tasks were parceled out to women or the checks handed over by them to the pastor without a thought that, having earned the money, members should be consulted about how it should be spent.

After listening to a woman's informed opinion, how often have I heard that same woman say, "But of course, I'm just a housewife, Father. Whatever you think is best."

I wonder how different it would have been if these women had known that the gift of prophecy, considered by many to be the highest form of ministry, was once exercised freely by women, women like Philip the evangelist's daughters who not only prophesied but also prayed aloud.[5]

Over the years, as I experienced the rhythms of family life, the births and deaths, the joys and humiliations, how comforted I could have been with the retelling of the stories of women who surrounded Jesus in his personal life, his human struggle. When my family needed me to be strong and courageous for them, I could have looked to the women who were there for Jesus at the time of his execution and burial: "Some women were there, looking on from a distance. Among them were Mary Magdalene, Mary the mother of the younger James and of Joseph, and Salome. They had followed Jesus while he was in Galilee and had helped him" (Mark 15:40-41).

I need to see them even now, not as a group of frightened, insecure women huddled in a web of fear, but as women of courage and daring whose overwhelming love for their Lord empowered them to risk their lives and reputations in order to embrace him with their presence and support.

I need to be dazzled by the fact that Jesus was not afraid to give and receive love from women, to acknowledge his dependence on them, or to entrust to them the knowledge of who he was and why he was there.

And when I feel diminished and humiliated by others, I need to remember that he never would have said: "You can't trust a woman" because "women can't keep secrets." Nor would Jesus have referred to women as "dumb blondes."

I think of the decades of Easters in which I sat listening but never questioning the words "But because they were women, no one believed them." Then I wonder how much that mind-set contributed to my self-definition as a woman in the church.

As the discussion regarding women's ordination mounts and the controversies flare, I need to recall how important the deaconesses were in the centuries of the early church. I need to keep remembering how crucial they were to the church in the area of ministry to women, how they cared for all women and assisted at their baptisms. Oh yes, we need them, these women! We need them to reach across the oceans and valleys of time to minister, by their example, to men and women, to daughters and sons, to me.

With my Hispanic sisters, I need to know more about such women as Sor Juana Inez de la Cruz, a Mexican nun of the seventeenth century, considered one of the leading feminists of the Americas. Sister Juana recognized the oppressions and limitations that women faced and chose to enter a Catholic cloister in lieu of living in a society that would force her to accept her fate passively.

From her cloister cell came the earliest written proclamations in defense of women as intellectual equals with men. Her argument was that the powers, virtues, and strengths of women were not visible because society had not permitted them to express themselves.[6]

I need to fashion new necklaces composed of the jeweled legacies of women whom I must summon up out of the mists of time to refute, once and for all, the charges that women are unable, unwilling, or uncomfortable to cope with the burdens and responsibilities of leadership in ministry.

I know now that men, as well as women, need models of women ministers. Men in the church, as well as women, suffer from this deprivation of the female witness in ministry.

I can only anticipate the excitement of the deeply spiritual young feminists I know when they discover the witness given by the remarkable women abbesses of the middle ages. These women exercised quasi-episcopal jurisdiction, both temporal and spiritual, and answered directly to Rome.[7]

I think of highly competent women theologians who need, in their struggle to obtain placement in seminary faculties, to be reminded of women like Saint Hilda of Whitby. She, we are told, was responsible for the spiritual training of her clergy, many of whom became bishops.[8]

And when women, in and out of the church, are told that they are not emotionally capable of running corporate structures, they must remember women like the Abbess Jeanne-Baptiste de Bourbon of the Abbey of Fontevrault. She was responsible for the nomination of her clergy, for the payment of benefices for their forty rectories, chapels, and churches, and for the nomination of the one hundred prioresses who were dependent on the centralized government of the abbey. The abbesses (not the bishops or priests) personally selected their priors, empowering them with the necessary license to preach, to confess, and to serve women's houses. In addition, they authorized confessors to absolve cases normally reserved to bishops.[9]

When pastors struggle with the concept of team ministry, they should be reminded that in these historical settings "priests and monks, together with the nuns, took vows of obedience to the abbess, in imitation of the obedience of Jesus to his mother, while the abbesses, in imitation of Mary, served the community devotedly in an administrative capacity."[10]

As women sit separated on the other side of the altar, whether at Mass or at ordinations, they should remember that it was not always so, that abbesses were, in fact, once ordained, replete with the symbols of episcopal office. They received and wore the mitre, crozier, ring, stole, alb, gloves, and pectoral cross.[11]

When Christian feminists fight against their non-presence in the power struggle, they should be encouraged by the knowledge that in the twelfth century, women not only convoked and presided at church synods but also emerged as the main leaders in discussions and as outstanding promoters of liturgical reform.[12]

In the tenth and eleventh centuries the power of the abbesses of the chief houses in Germany, those of Quedlinburg and Gandershein, were able, under Otto I, to strike their own coins bearing their portraits.[13]

The divine office was chanted by women in the dual cathedrals, and abbesses presided at all their own church services, except the eucharist, for which they were not ordained.[14] The Abbess of Quedlinburg had both a seat and a vote on the Imperial Diet,[15] while the English abbesses were called to Parliament during the twelfth century.[16] The privilege of observer status accorded to women at the Second Vatican Council is a mockery when compared to the enormous political power enjoyed by these medieval women.

When women today note that they, like many of their daughters, were allowed to function only as flower girls in church processions (unless one was lucky enough to be the May Queen and to crown the Blessed Mother), they should be told that once "canonnesses walked in front of clergy carrying the pastoral cross."[17] They lived and breathed, these women, exercising incalculable influence, touching lives, healing souls, making decisions.

"At one time, it [women's leadership in the church] was enjoyed and desired by all people," historian Joan Morris tells us. "Today it is hidden history, hardly believed and not understood."[18] We marvel today at the seemingly few solitary survivors, the women whose influence was so overwhelming that not even the oversights or outright abolitions of church historians could dim the lustre of their lives.

They stand tall and splendid, untarnished in their undisputed witness: women like Saint Catherine of Siena and Saint Teresa of Avila, both recently granted the official title of Doctor of the

Church. How they labored and traveled and struggled! As I come to know them, I realize how much during my lifetime I would have turned to them, prayed to them to help me as I labored (with my toddlers), traveled (in my never-ending carpools), and struggled as they did to be listened to, to be heard.

When there was never enough money, enough time, enough energy, how much I would have loved Teresa's words when she was asked to make two new foundations. She said, "I had no means for making either, but that was no disadvantage as I generally began with less than nothing."[19] And yet, her value of woman, as person, was still diminished. "That woman," sighed her bishop of Teresa, "should have been a man."[20]

I cannot help but think, too, how many of our sad-eyed sons and daughters of the sixties, in search of their wholeness, would have been strengthened and comforted by the remarkable revelations of the fourteenth-century mystic, Julian of Norwich, writing, as she did, of the *motherhood* of God:

> As truly as God is our Father, so truly is God our Mother. . . . Jesus is our true Mother in nature by our first creation and he is our true Mother in grace by his taking our created nature. . . . The Mother's service is nearest, readiest, surest; nearest, because it is most natural, readiest because it is the most loving, and surest because it is truest. . . . We know that all our mothers bear us for pain and for death. . . . But our true Mother Jesus, he alone bears us for joy and for endless life. . . . The mother can give her child to suck of her milk but our precious Mother Jesus can feed us with himself and does, most courteously and tenderly with the Blessed Sacrament, which is the precious food of true life. . . . The Mother can lay her child tenderly to her breast, but our tender Mother Jesus can lead us easily into his blessed breast through his sweet open side and show us there a part of the godhead and of the joys of heaven, with inner

certainty of endless bliss. . . . To the property of motherhood belong nature, love, wisdom and knowledge and this is
God. For though it may be so that our bodily bringing to
birth is only little, humble and simple in comparison with
our spiritual bringing to birth, still it is he who does it in the
creatures by whom it is done.[21]

I wonder, too, in what ways these same young idealists of the
sixties might have done things differently if, sitting around their
commune campfires, they had known some challenging models
of community to draw upon like the Beguines of the twelfth
century. They were women who established houses on the out-
skirts of towns in Belgium and lived semi-monastic lives. They
devoted themselves to the care of the poor and infirm.

Although they chose to live in community, Beguines could
not be considered nuns. They took no vows and could return to
the world and marry if they chose to. They did not, upon
entering, renounce their property. They supported themselves by
teaching or by manual labor and neither requested nor accepted
alms. Each Beguine was bound to her community by a common
purpose, mutual pursuits, and a common worship. There was no
motherhouse, nor common rule, nor common general order;
every community was complete in itself and fixed in its own
order.

Foundations were established in Germany, England, and
France. By the end of the thirteenth century, practically every
town had at least one beguinage. Several, like the Great
Beguinage at Ghent, numbered their inhabitants by the
thousands. As centers of mysticism, they greatly influenced the
religious life of the people, superseding the monks and the
secular clergy in moulding the thought of the urban population
of the Netherlands.[22] The Great Beguinage at Ghent, surrounded by its walls and moats, contained at the beginning of

the fourteenth century two churches, eighteen convents, over one-hundred houses, a brewery, and an infirmary.

The beguinage, described as an attempt to harmonize the individual and the communal in the Middle Ages, was actually a town on a miniature scale with the church as the hub.[23]

They are all gone now, these women, swept under by the tidal wave of history, with all its contradictions, their power and glory gradually receding over the centuries like a slowly ebbing tide.

But nothing of truth is lost forever.

One day we walk along a familiar shore strewn with seaweed, grateful if we can be rewarded with the sight of even a single shell from the sea. We search idly through the tangle and web of the ocean's uprooted garden, only to be surprised by the sight of a thousand emeralds, a buried treasure, that has somehow, suddenly, been washed ashore.

CHAPTER TWO

Where Are Women Today?
Questions and Options

TODAY'S WOMEN ARE CAUGHT in the eye of a storm. Many of them are there by choice, but most have been swept up into its center by culture and circumstances. Not even those who have boarded their windows and doors against its fury have remained untouched by its battering. For somehow, the storm, which began out there as "somebody else's problem," now seems to be raging, however imperceptibly, in the hearts of women everywhere.

The storm's devastation is achingly familiar; its refugees are everywhere. In its wake, it has left children without parents, parents without partners, and a society running in circles in search of itself.

Lightning first struck when women began asking uncomfortable questions—questions like, "Who says I can't?" and "Why shouldn't I?" (Two out of three marriages could not survive the aftershock.)

But slowly, women started answering their own questions. They learned that they could turn their time and talent into paychecks. They let existing social justice legislation lean on doors for them until the doors opened to let them in. They went from lighting fires at family hearths to lighting them under the legislature. They turned a lifetime of "whys?" into "why nots?"

And the questions kept coming along with the answers. Many of them came just by listening. Women began listening to one another. Mothers and daughters began challenging each other's ideas around the dinner tables, while husbands and fathers and sons sat back, suddenly looking at women with new eyes. Soon psychologists, physicians, social and behavioral scientists, politicians listened as women not only told where they hurt but why.

PTAs began to examine textbook stereotyping; women started to realize that the Equal Opportunity Employer had to deal with the issue of a person's sex as much as with the color of a person's skin. Volunteer groups like the Junior Leagues of America began to set up procedures to aid their members in assigning a cash value to their proven executive leadership in the community when applying for paid employment in the labor market. Widows and divorcees began to appear on talk shows to discuss their books and/or their problems. Funding materialized for rape centers as well as shelters for battered women and children from every segment of society.

And from the uterus out, everything about women's bodies came under scrutiny, both sexually and politically.

Inevitably, women came to see themselves as both economic units and power brokers: studies were conducted on the unpaid services of the homemaker; surveys were taken on women's satisfaction with their media image; children were tested on the emotional side effects of having working mothers; men were interviewed on their flexibility in becoming house-husbands; young executives were questioned about their psychological security in relocating so their wives could get a better job.

Aware now of their power as consumers, women suddenly discovered that they had another power: the power of *not* spending money. Thousands joined in the economic boycott of states that refused to pass the Equal Rights Amendment. Women began demanding accountability from the male-dominated medical profession, questioning everything from safety in birth control and childbirth at home to the mass dispensation of tranquilizers which so often had led to legal drug addiction for many women.

And despite the image of the women's movement as being one of middle-class professional women, virtually all of the thousands of sex-discrimination complaints filed with the Equal Employment Opportunity Commission under the Civil Rights Act have been filed by women factory and clerical workers. The millions of dollars in back pay that have been paid to women under the Equal Pay Act have mainly gone to non-professional women.[1]

It should have come as no surprise to the institutional church that their day of challenge by women was inevitable. In churches all over America, a quiet revolution was taking place. Increasingly, women began realizing that though they comprised over half the membership, they had no voice, no vote, no recourse to the fact that they were totally without legal representation. When they pleaded their case, they were told that the laws could not be changed without violating "tradition," which is another way of saying that men would continue making all the decisions governing them.

"Why," women asked, "am I able to receive more equity in civil society, in the pagan marketplace, than in the church that speaks to me of justice and charity, honesty and accountability?"

The church, for all intents and purposes, simply shrugged.

A few words were put on paper, a few committees hastily assembled, but women began to realize that it would take eons for the massive mound of church bureaucracy to rouse itself, to breathe itself to new conclusions, new history.

The only problem was that while the church was the same, women had changed. Now imbued with a growing sense of their own self-dignity and worth as persons and affirmed by forces around them, they had to accept the fact that they were not being taken seriously.

And so the women who formerly baked the cookies, sold the raffle tickets, organized the rummage sales, and built the schools now began to express their disappointment in the institutional church in the public forum. Others chose to demonstrate their dissatisfaction and anger by simply staying away.

If this trend continues, the church will find itself essentially immobilized. And now we are at the heart of it, the pulse of the storm, for it is from this point that all the currents of our lives converge. We may control our money, our bodies, our behavior, and our labor, but if we go thirsty at the wellspring of the spirit, then all of us, men and women alike, will pass into that final grayness which is a life without God.

We have come to a time of trembling, of holy questioning about who we are and who we should become, for ourselves as well as for others. This is not a question simply of women's rights but of the future of humankind: the future of person, of marriage, of family, of community. But it is important to remember that all honest questioning should be without terror, for though questions imply risk, risk leads to growth, and growth is the promise of new life.

It is also important to know that we are not alone. Christ, too, came to ask questions and the answers he gave also made people uncomfortable, especially when those answers called them to accept new challenges.

That is why it has become critical to proceed lovingly, *loving ourselves* enough to become courageous, knowing that we are moving towards Christ's promise of why he came, why he took the risk *for us*. "I have come," he said, "in order that you might have life—life in all its fullness" (Jn 10:10).

So although we tremble at the threshold of our questions, we should proceed with confidence, knowing from our life experience alone that we can accept the responsibility of any surprises we may uncover. We, who have so often had our sensitivity used against us, ("Women are so emotional!") should now see sensitivity as a strength. Because we see that the church is losing its women, it is we who must stand up and ask for accountability, for we have come to a time in which our spiritual future is in the balance.

Perhaps what we most need is the courage to be patient, to shut out all the sounds which surround us so that we can at last listen to a single voice, a voice we can no longer ignore and must learn to trust.

That voice is our own.

Requiem

She longed to be buried in the white silk of old age,
    in the wisdom that only the ancient years
    call forth from the heart.
She longed to be loved
    as a body outside herself could be loved,
as a body which is part of something other than a name,
    or a face.

Many years passed by, making the woman more lonely.
Different men came to her, made love to her,
    & left her alone, with only their scent
    still upon her body.

She would weep, not just for herself,
    but for all the alone things that she knew of . . . . [1]

Thomas Roberdeau

CHAPTER THREE

Where Should Women Begin?
The Body as Battleground

"A fundamental challenge for women assuming responsibility for ministry in the Roman Catholic church is leadership in reclaiming for the whole church a ministry in the flesh. . . . it can best be realized through the witness and wisdom of women who have known such deep wounds because of their flesh."[1]

Sister M. Timothy Prokes, SSND

SHE STANDS ALONE BEFORE a three-way mirror, her coat securely buttoned, a scarf nearly enveloping her head and face.

The room is bare except for a stream of slanted sunlight which comes through the single window, the silence tattooed by the sound of a softly ticking clock hidden somewhere. But she is without fear, because she knows she is dreaming. If she were awake, she would never have had the courage to make the trip, as she knew she must, alone.

She lifts her head and meets her eyes in the mirror straight ahead of her. She sees a woman in her forties, a woman whose gaze is clear but whose eyes are waiting. Slowly, she unwinds her scarf and removes it. Carefully, she removes her coat, allowing it to fall upon the floor.

She sees the outline of a body, her reality. (Why, then, do her fingers suddenly reach up and touch her cheeks as if to reassure herself of something?)

"See," she smiles to the reflection. "See, I told you you were not invisible. Even when you doubted it, I always knew that you were there!"

She glances at her triple reflection in the mirror. To the left, she sees her mother (with messages about what it is to be a woman—the scripts, so many of which have now become self-fulfilling). To the right, she sees her daughter (at once, her student and her teacher, a series of silken cords to be cut and refashioned, one by one). She sees them, but she cannot touch them. She can only touch herself here, and she has only now.

She looks again into the middle mirror, overwhelmed with a sudden weariness. "Why do I feel suspended between the strengths of these women on either side of me? Why do I feel so pockmarked with guilt, so nibbled away at the edges? Why does being a woman mean never being *enough*, somehow?"

Not why, but why not?

To find the answer, she will have to stand before that mirror, before her mother and her daughter, naked. She will have to shed her questions, her burdens, one by one. She will have to look at her body slowly, carefully (for once, without guilt, without shame, without fear of punishment). She has nothing but time now to ask herself how she feels about what she sees. It is a question she is not accustomed to asking.

For centuries, the question has been asked and answered for her by others—primarily the wise and good and holy men in the church. They have described her, defined her, instructed her, legislated for her without ever once consulting her. ("What do you need? How do you feel? What do you think?") Apparently, they never thought her reality was important enough to warrant seeking her input. Her worth was seen in terms of whom those churchmen needed her *to be* (servant, laborer, domestic) *for them*.

She realizes now that it was a setup for schizophrenia. Officially, the churchmen demanded that she be saintly and emulate the Blessed Virgin, but theologically, in eliminating her from the decision-making process and in describing her as "defective male"[2] and "full of filth,"[3] she was imaged, historically, as everything from a simpleton to a whore.

But the woman in the mirror, while growing up, of course, never knew that. The messages she had received about her body were quite uncomplicated. Her body was where she lived and what she walked around in. And as she grew, she knew she was supposed to keep it covered and never "touch" it—*ever*. And as the years passed, and as her breasts swelled (or failed to swell) beneath her high-school sweater, she hunched her shoulders and tried to hide what was happening because (either way) she felt ashamed.

There were, of course, other legacies, like Sister telling her that, as a woman, she should be "careful" of her body and "protect" it. (Sister was, of course, the perfect, if impossible example, swathed as she was from head to toe in flowing veils.) But deep down, she knew that being careful was not so much a message to protect herself as it was to "protect" the boys.

Growing up, she knew there were so many things to remember that "good girls" never did; there were so many garden varieties of shame. There was the shame of her body, the shame of menstruation, that bright red stain that spread across her mind as well as her body. (Were cramps part of the "punishment," imagined or real?) She remembers her friend Angie telling her that she went to bed with "the curse" every month because she thought being "sick" was a *normal* part of having a monthly period. She remembers worrying about whether she was ever "clean enough" to cover up her dirty secret. (God forbid that the boys should suspect she was "on the rag," much less know!)

"Our feelings about menstruation are the image of what it is to be a woman in this culture," Nancy Friday writes, remembering the advertisements for sanitary napkins that were part of her conditioning as a woman as she grew up.[4] "What have we to do with those beautiful women, gowned by Givenchy, stepping out of limousines in the Modess Because...advertisements," she wonders.[5] They were so marvelous, so ethereal, so untouchable, so *white*! How could the woman in the mirror ever forget them? She knew they had to be exempt from anything so vile as bloody sanitary napkins.

And so she looked at those beautiful ladies and fantasized her fears away, denying, negating her bodily reality. For she knew that underneath the gowns billowing with layers of tulle and taffeta, these women were unsoiled, unspotted, sweet smelling. So once again her insecurity about her body was reinforced; she purchased products for her body, a victim once again of "hard-sell shame."

And yet, standing there before the mirror, the woman wonders: *What about my brother and his body? Was he ever punished for his wet dreams? Did he live in constant fear of being "smelly" from his genitals? of feeling that being a man made him "unclean"?*

But growing pains were not confined to menstruation, she remembers. For girls, there was the shame of the confessional, the shame of the soul, the hot shame heightened by the pastor's icy reminder that "if girls get in trouble, it's their own fault, isn't it? After all, a boy only goes as far as a girl allows." And since boys get "worked up" faster than girls do, then she was guilty not only of impurity but also of cruelty in "leading him on." Did this mean that men were not morally accountable or simply that, despite their seeming "manhood," they had no control whatever over their own lives?

After marriage, of course, the heat was turned up on the thermostat, and shame became intensified by guilt.

She looks now at her body in the mirror: the curve of her breasts, the roundness of her hips, the white softness of her abdomen above the patch of pubic hair. Was it a thousand years ago that that body trembled in confusion on her wedding night? After a lifetime of "No!" it was suddenly supposed to be transformed into a technicolor "Yes!" Sometimes, it was. But even then, down deep in her heart of hearts, she felt frozen in her free, floating body, wondering whether she would, in fact, still be punished if she completely "let go."

Jessie Potter says that if we can repress a girl enough about her genitals:

> she'll never find them. Even if she does, she is going to have had so many negative messages, she will have been anesthetized from her knees to her belly button. After we've taught her that part of her body is so awful, you can't even call it by name, that it smells bad and she'd better not even look at it, then we tell her she must save it for the man she loves, women must be pardoned for being less than enthusiastic about such a gift.[6]

The woman looks now in the mirror to the left of her and studies her mother: the sweet, round face etched with age and the fine gray hair fanning out softly from her trusting face. The woman is overwhelmed, once again, with an ache, a longing to touch her, to talk to her, to give and receive comfort from this woman who, above all others, was the first artist to sketch out her daughter's destiny.

"Long before the lectures, the book left on the bedside table, the film at school, we have learned about our sexuality from mother's denials, avoidance and her relationship to her own body."[7]

"Oh Mother," she calls to the image reflected back at her. "Mother . . . Mother . . . there were so many things we needed to heal in one another. There were so many gifts we had in common that we didn't know how to celebrate! Of all the books of poetry on your bedside table, was there ever a copy of the Song of Songs (Canticle of Canticles)? Or did you hide it, like I hid behind my questions, knowing that there would only be an agony of embarrassment if I asked you things too 'indelicate' to answer?"

Thy two breasts are more beautiful than wine and the
  sweet smell of thy ointments above all aromatical
  spices...
Thy belly is like a heap of wheat, set about with lilies...
The joints of thy thighs are like jewels...
  (Cant. 4:10, 7:2, 7:1—Douay).

There were so many books they might have shared, initially
as literature, like the one which declared that in Rabbinic Juda-
ism, the Talmud encouraged the devout to begin the Sabbath by
reading from the Song of Songs and engaging in the marital act
on the premise that these practices would stimulate a more
joyous disposition for worship: "When the Sabbath comes, it is
incumbent on them to *gladden their wives* for the sake of the
honor of the Heavenly Partner."[8]

"Would that have made it easier?" she wonders aloud to her
mother's silent reflection. "Would we have seen ourselves as
more than mother and daughter? Would we have learned to love
ourselves first as healthy, sensual women?"

Instinctively, she looks to the right, to the image of her
daughter's reflection. She sees a young woman on the edge of
twenty, watching, listening, waiting. What has she taught *her*
about being a woman? What filtered through the memories, the
stories of growing up in the forties and fifties as a "good girl
from a nice, religious home"?

Instinctively, her hands touch her abdomen.

Standing before the mirror, she cannot see her uterus, but
she knows now it was always the site of her conscience. She
knew she, alone, had to bear the burden of responsibility for the
new life, or lack of it, which flourished there.

She remembers how quickly the babies flowered, one after
another, within that abdomen. She remembers the times she
turned away from her husband in fear and anxiety in the spaces
between those babies, the spectre of still another pregnancy

haunting their kisses and caresses, while she fought off the guilt of refusing her husband, of being "a good wife," no matter what that might entail.

After years of "rhythm" (ten years, five pregnancies), she offered her body up on what proved to be the altar of medical research; she took the pill. Suddenly it was a matter "between you and your husband!" priest after priest informed her. "Use your own conscience; *only you know what's best for you!*" But freedom, as any newly-released captive can tell you, is a bit more complicated than that. The Catholic woman's Declaration of Independence, she discovered, did not necessarily come in capsule form. Time after time, the gynecologist reached into his desk drawer for still another sample to "try out." Surely, among his chemical treasures, there would be one pill that would not make her bleed or vomit or hemorrhage or give her heart attacks or cause her to die.

She wonders now, how many men (besides convicts) ever felt desperate or, worse, indifferent enough to allow themselves to become pawns for the pharmaceutical industry (assuming, of course, that chemical, potentially harmful male contraceptives were even considered as a *priority* for research).

She smiles at the mirror wistfully. She realizes that she has never heard a woman speak of her body with *reverence*. She thinks of the crude words men use to refer to her vagina in contrast to their description of their genitals as "the family jewels." She wonders what it would be like to think so highly of her genitalia that she could glibly accuse men of vagina envy whenever they expressed the slightest anger or aggressiveness in professional or social situations.

> We never get over our worries about our waist and weight because they are not the real and unmentionable and unthinkable root of our concern. . . . We say it is our breasts and thighs that are ugly; we fear it is our vagina. . . . It's what

an analyst friend of mine calls "lack of vaginal self-respect". . . .

Why do we spend too much money on clothes, too many hours over facials? Because we can't believe anyone would want us as we are. Convince a woman that her vagina is beautiful and you have the makings of an "equal" person. I believe this with all my heart.[9]

"I wonder," she says aloud to her reflection, "how many priests, even today, counsel men to take up the 'burden' of family planning through the method of vasectomies? How many sermons are preached on nuptial co-responsibility. . .that while it's no news that 'a wife is not the master of her own body, but her husband is; in the same way, a husband is not the master of his own body, but his wife is' " (I Co 7:4).

Her mother would have shrugged or sighed or shaken her head had she heard that quotation, even from the pulpit. "Offer it up" was her abiding legacy, three words which formed a kind of theological umbrella. In that time and place, no one ever heard of questions; there were only endless pre-packaged answers: a baby a year was considered "a blessing"; sex was spoken of as "the marriage duty"; it was always assumed to be the wife's fault if the husband "strayed."

To live was to suffer. . .suffer! And soon, in her mind, suffering became so institutionalized, that it replaced religion as a woman's raison d'être—a woman who never reached Easter Sunday, because no one encouraged her to get her body down from the cross.

She looked at her mother in the mirror and remembered her funeral. How ironic that the priest should circle the casket and "bless" the body with prayers and incense! Where was the blessing, the incense, when she needed them, as a woman, a wife, a mother of daughters? What good did it do to give the body a *final* blessing in death when the church failed to celebrate that body when it was alive?

How long ago, it seems now, as faded as the rose petals they dropped as little girls in May processions. . . so long ago and yet, still here, enclosed within her body: all she was, is, and would one day be.

She looks at her body with curiosity that turns to wonder: at the arms that reached and hugged and held a family; at the breasts that nursed the hungry babies, the milk rising like a miracle, spilling instinctively from her nipples at the first sound of the baby's cry.

Her hands return to her abdomen, this time her fingers spreading as if to hold it, enclose it. She remembers the month-by-month awesomeness of pregnancy, the white skin stretching with the rising tummy, the fine veins visible like a fragile net holding a precious cargo.

She recalls the first feeling of life. . . the surprise, the delight, the wonder. . . the sound of the heartbeat through the stethoscope (could she distinguish between the baby's heartbeat and her own?). . . and finally the spiral of pain that she knew was the signal of labor. Each time, she instinctively reached for her prayer book, wondering on whose feast day this child would be born.

So many births, so many babies. . . so many months and years and minutes of carrying life, of giving birth to others. . . of *waiting* (for what?). . . expecting *something* (from whom?). . . of needing *more*. . . .

It is then that the sunlit, whitewashed room is filled with the sound of her voice crying out from deep within her. The sound is beyond words, beyond understanding, rushing past tears which stream from her eyes like a hidden wellspring, a sound that suddenly fills the empty room.

She calls out her own name over and over. . . until the room overflows with it and echoes. She is calling herself into being. She is giving herself rebirth.

Wake up, North Wind.
South Wind, blow on my garden;
fill the air with fragrance.
How beautiful you are, my love;
how perfect you are! (Sgs 4:16,7)

Is it birth or resurrection? She knows only that her voice is clear and unmistakable and steady and that she is standing *strong*.
"Naked and alone we came into exile."[10]
She looks at the soft pile of clothes which she dropped on the floor when she came here. But she knows now that she has outgrown them. Like her old scripts, they are dated; like her former doubts and fears, they are faded. She has moved to another place now, a new plateau, away from that airless hut she called her ego, that place only large enough to crawl into, that space where once she had to huddle to keep warm.

As silver is tried by fire, and gold in the furnace,
so the Lord trieth the hearts (Prov. 17:3—Douay).

She sinks to her knees now and sits back on her heels, her arms wrapped round her.
"Oh God," she cries softly, "is this what I needed to do to know how strong I am, to see myself as a survivor? Is this what it took to grow beyond the scar tissue, the anger, the answers that have lost their meaning? Is this what I had to do, as a woman, to find you, to reclaim your strength in me, to feel the breath of *your* life, which set my pulse in motion within my mother's womb?"
She turns now to her daughter's reflection in the mirror. She longs to call her into the room. "Look at me!" she whispers

softly. "I am part of your past and some of your future. I ask only that you pause and consider my legacies.

"I gave you a Bible but I never told you that the Good News begins in your body...it *is* your body! I never told you your Baptism *included* your body, with all its contours and folds and hidden wonders. Your body was given as a gift, not punishment. Learn to know it and love it, to touch it with joy and reverence as you would a holy thing.

"Praise God for the curve of your mouth, the span of your hips, the arch of your feet, the symmetry of your separate toes. Everything about your body *belongs to you* and should be *cherished*. There are no secret places to be avoided, to be ashamed of, to be hidden. To believe that is to say that God made some kind of terrible mistake in your design.

"It was he who fashioned your body with all the miracles contained within it: the sound of laughter that wells up from your throat, the tears which baptize your joy and pain. It was he who decided that there should be, within your body, the gift of orgasm, that sweet, sudden shuddering rising from your vagina, filling your whole being with intense delight.

> I opened the bolt of my door to my beloved
> ...My soul melted when he spoke...
> My beloved put his hands through the keyhole
> and my bowels were moved at his touch.
> I arose to open to my beloved
> ...and my fingers were full of the choicest myrrh
> (Cant. 5:6,4,5—Douay).

We are his *creation*. He designed us *to be* (feel, respond) the way *he* wanted us to be! He sees our bodies as beautiful! Why can't we?

"He illuminates his own incarnation when he tells us: 'I came that they might have life, and have it to the full' (Jn 10:10). For women, what does that mean? *It means that we live in God fully in our womanhood.*

" 'God created human beings, making them to be like Himself. He created them male and female. . .' (Gn 1:27). Our bodies are just as surely bonded to his as are those of our brothers. In this light, women's blood, which includes menstrual blood, can only be sacred (never profane!) for this blood, too, is 'in His image and likeness.' Women's blood is always sacred, whether it is poured out in life (childbirth) or, in accordance with divine design, in menstruation, referred to in at least one graceful instance as 'the tears of the disappointed womb.'

"Women should remember this particularly at Mass when the host is raised and they hear the words 'This is my body, this is my blood.' They share deeply in those words of consecration in their own bodies. Further, women are able to enter into the Eucharist by laying additional claim to a flesh-and-blood consecration from their own life experience in childbearing. What is childbirth if not a literal offering up of one's body and blood for another? As the fruit of that offering, what is a newborn child but a kind of resurrection of the human race through rebirth? Indeed, what actually transpires during the nine-month gestation which occurs during pregnancy but a gradual transformation of the mother's bread and wine (food and drink) into body and blood (Eucharist) in the form of another human being?

" 'Jesus came to bring life more abundantly, transforming what it meant to be human, breaking open the potential of lived body in ways unforeseen.'[11] Women's blood is as precious to the Lord as his is to women. Were it not so, he would not have risked scandal by ministering to a woman afflicted with bleeding in a culture which ostracized women for their natural bodily functions by labeling them ritually impure. Teilhard de Chardin reminds us that 'by virtue of creation and still more of the incarnation, *nothing* here below *is profane* for those who know how to see.'[12]

"And so, my daughter, perhaps that is the first task: to look, not to notice, but to *see*. We must begin to see our bodies as grace-filled, grace-full. Mary Ann Finch, a teacher of Bodily Theology, helps us begin. 'I minister, first of all, to myself and then I minister to others, trying to create a harmony between their mind, their body and their spirit.'[13]

"Thou shalt love thy neighbor *as thyself*. For many women, ministering to themselves through accepting and celebrating their bodies will be the first step toward ministering to others with a new kind of integrity: the respect for a person's wholeness (holiness?), which embraces body and soul. It is the kind of ministry which reflects the love of a God who 'saw all things that he had made and they were very good' (Gen. 1:31—Douay).

"To do this, we women must struggle against the sovereigns and scripts of church history whose negative messages about women (which include her non-presence) were rooted and written in fear.

> The prevailing Biblical outlook on matrimonial intercourse stands in bold relief against the persistent sexophobia of church history. Had it not been regarded as pure, the Hebrew prophets and the apostle Paul would not have used sexual metaphors in their theology. . . . Had the apostle thought sex was dirty, he would not have summed up his discussions of sexual morality in these words: "your body is the temple of the Holy Spirit. . . so use your bodies for God's glory" (I Cor 6:19–20).[14]

But how can this happen when people are 'out of touch' with their bodies?

"Speaking of her ministry, Mary Ann Finch says,

> If I could heal one hurt, perhaps it would be the loneliness. People have a tremendous fear of their bodies, the avenue through which they experience being human. When they are

not at home with that, then humanness is something that is not fulfilling. There is no way they can understand the meaning of a relationship, the meaning of God.[15]

"We need only recall the words of Scripture: 'Choose life, so that you and your descendants might live' (Deut. 30:19—Douay). To be *alive*, my daughter, is in itself a gift, a celebration of the senses. To inhale the fragrance of lilacs, to touch the bark of an ancient redwood tree, to feel the warmth of the morning sun! But to be alive to the *source* of one's gifts, alive to the body which is the fountain of all our sensory perceptions, is to be in touch with the pulse of the Spirit from whom we receive every feeling which floods our being.

"How can a body which whirls to a Strauss waltz or balances on a pair of skis or strokes another's brow in tenderness be anything but awesome? Why do we spend so much energy distrusting it, abusing it, discounting it? What does this say about our attitude towards its Creator? What, indeed, would we say to him about our bodies if he were here? '*Lord, my smile is too radiant, my nipples too erotic, my fingers too flexible, my skin too supple, my eyelashes too long!*'

"How can we even talk about ministry, about reconciling, nourishing, comforting, unless we truly love and trust and dignify our body, the instrument through which we expect to minister and heal? How can we hope to cherish others if we do not love ourselves?

"Sister Timothy Prokes reminds us that 'It means receiving all embodiment as gift and knowing that gift ever more intimately as way of relationship. It means being poured out in the flesh in thanksgiving as fundamental to Christian ministry.'[16]

"But there is another dimension women bring to ministry through their bodies, a dimension the Spirit is calling out of them from their own life-experience, a dimension of ministry whose time has come. For women who have suffered and struggled within the flesh precisely as it expresses their uniqueness as women, it is significant that ministry is lived through the body-persons of 'wounded healers.'[17] The possibilities for women to minister in this capacity in prisons and rape centers alone is staggering!

"Mary Ann Finch reminds us that Jesus, in his ministry to people, did not begin by touching souls; *he touched bodies.* And through bodies, these people begin to experience wholeness. Jesus really affirmed the body. The miracle began with the body and then that health penetrated into the spirit of a person.[18]

"But as usual, Jesus not only told us, he showed us, careful, always, in his humanity, to ask nothing of us that he himself was not willing to show us how to do.

> Then Mary took a whole pint of very expensive perfume made of pure nard, poured it on Jesus' feet, and wiped them with her hair. The sweet smell of the perfume filled the whole house (Jn 12:3).

But Jesus not only received Mary's ministry, he praised it highly. He did in fact accord her, a woman, the highest praise he ever gave to *any* human being in the recorded Gospel,[19] and it occurred at the moment he received the *physical* manifestation of her love: 'Now remember this! "Wherever the gospel is preached all over the world, what she has done will be told in memory of her" ' (Mk 14:9). By massaging his feet, a sensual act in itself, Mary ministered to Jesus physically as well as spiritually, with the tenderness of her touch. And in receiving her gift and praising her for it, he was giving us a double message: not only that he accepted a gift from her body to his body but also that he acknowledged the gift to be so important that he wanted the world to remember it for all time. What clearer message could he give us about our bodies?

"It is no wonder that Mary Ann Finch exclaims, 'As a minister, I feel it is my responsibility to help people to pass into their bodies and to accept them and to say, "Well, there's really nothing to feel guilty about!" '[20]

"The Word was made Flesh"!

And now the room is silent. The woman is aware of the mirrors on either side of her, of the images of her mother and her daughter, and then of a gradual shimmering.

Suddenly, their reflections have receded. She is alone. But there is a difference now. In the middle mirror straight ahead of her she does not see herself; there is a new reflection. She sees the lined face of a woman bending with age, although her body swells with pregnancy.

It is Elizabeth, Mary's cousin, calling to her across the centuries, greeting her, once more, through all the Marys, all the mothers that brought her, finally, to her own mother. It is Elizabeth, kinswoman to all women, reminding her that age is no barrier to giving birth, in mind or body. "For there is nothing that God cannot do" (Lk 1:37).

CHAPTER FOUR

What Do Women Fear?

Stumbling Blocks to Self-Definition

"All of the women I know feel a little like outlaws."[1]
Marilyn French

MARTHA ANAYA AND ANITA
Mendoza are nineteen-year-old Latino career girls who share a
similar childhood memory of the Catholic Church. At different
times and in different places, they saw no reason why their sex
prevented them from full participation at Sunday Mass. Anita
remembers asking if she could be the priest in a dramatization of
the Mass in catechism class. Martha informed her parents that
she planned "to ask Father if I can be an altar girl." In both cases,
the nine-year-old girls were actively discouraged. One has memories of being ridiculed.

"I felt I had done something terrible," Anita said, "and all
these years, I have carried a hurt and an anger inside me, wishing,
as I did then, that there was someone who could explain to me
what I'd done wrong."

Martha's memories, on the other hand, caused her to be
more and more aware of what she calls "the male witness. It's
emphasized in the scripture readings, in the absence of women
on the altar, in sermons which are always presented from a male
point of view. I keep asking myself: *Where are the women? They
love Jesus and want to witness to him. Don't they qualify as
Christians, too?"*

• Lollie Lorentz is one of the parish "regulars" at daily Mass. The petite fifty-eight-year-old grandmother not only grew up and was married in that parish, but she brought up and schooled all her five children there as well.

A faith-filled woman who sees only positives in terms of her past church life, Lollie nevertheless admits that today she feels more of a "sentimental attachment" to the church rather than the sense of commitment she had in former days.

Noting that she would be at a loss to know how to attract anyone to Catholicism, she said simply, "I wouldn't know what to say to impress them. I guess I can see through so many things now . . . things like the authority question. And I see the need my daughters and granddaughters have for women models in the church to relate to. But there aren't any women there!"

• "When you say the words 'Catholic woman' to me," says vibrant, intelligent Kim Averie, a twenty-five-year-old film pro-duction assistant, "my word associations are *misplaced, clamp-down* and *second hand.*"

After eight years of Catholic schooling, Kim sees "a basic dichotomy in a church which foists male priest-counselors on women after training priests to distrust women as 'dangerous occasions of sin.'

"As a young girl, I remember wishing I could find something in my religion which would help me to feel more comfortable with myself and give me confidence to relate to the outside world. But I guess that was unrealistic in a school where boys and girls couldn't speak to each other at recess after the fifth grade."

• For Fran Farber, newly divorced and mother of three, time is running out.

"For twenty years, I've fought the good fight. I've supported Catholic schools while I taught CCD on Saturday. I've organized rummage sales and card parties; I've celebrated liturgies and loved the church with all my energy. Now, suddenly, I'm a divorcee, someone on the outside, with only a neat little label defining my identity.

"I keep looking for a gesture of understanding, knowing that I'm now one of thousands who must turn elsewhere in search of a life line to some sort of caring Christian community.

"It's a lonely place to be when you're a mother," she said, "but I'm hopeful. I have great trust in the timetable of a loving God. Someday when the church gets closer to Christ, there'll be room for all women. Even," she said softly, "for women like me."

• "I see myself, not as a 'Catholic mother,' but as part of a continuing tradition which includes scripture and history," says Dr. Terry Johnston, a clinical and community psychologist and mother of eleven children, three of whom are girls.

"But the church today is not living up to Christianity, because it has allowed itself to become encrusted with irrelevancies and is twenty years behind the times. Consequently, it says little to young people and it will continue to lose them as long as it looks at the world with 'one eye.' "

From a professional point of view, Dr. Johnston said that she sees the church negatively in terms of most of her women clients. She relates the comment of one such woman who said in painful jest, "Do I feel guilty? I was born guilty. I was born a Catholic."

What does it mean to be "born a Catholic"? From what theological cocoon has the Catholic woman emerged? Growing up, who were her models as women? What kind of messages did she receive from them about who she was supposed to be?

If she grew up before the sixties, she sat, as a child, in a hushed church peering up at the looming statues: figures of women swathed in flowing robes, their faces upturned and angelic, portraits of both mysterious rapture and indefinable pain. Often their faces were bandaged roundabout with strange headdresses, not unlike the kind the nuns wore, leaving only a pale face visible, dominated by imploring eyes.

Sometimes her young eyes rested on a statue, a portion of whose body was bleeding: the heart encircled with thorns or the open wounds in hands and feet, which indicated the stigmata of a saint. One can only wonder now at the impressions that formed in her young mind.

The women in the statues seemed strange and somewhat scary. They certainly weren't like the women she knew in the neighborhood or saw in the market. They weren't like her aunties, her mother, her sisters. But everyone said they were holy and beautiful. She wondered how she could be like them so that people would call her holy, too.

She thought a lot about the saint her mother told her she'd been named for. She was a woman known for her obedience and humility. "Mind you, you've got a lot of virtues to live up to," her mother told her. Again, she wondered how she could ever measure up.

The only other women she could turn to were the nuns, her teachers. How awesome and serene they were, gliding along in graceful, floor-length habits forever fragrant with the smell of starch and soap. They were different, somehow puzzling. She noticed it when Daddy and Mother stepped back and lowered their voices when they talked to them. Whatever Sister said was the last word, final. There was no way she could be wrong. Even when she bent over a desk to help with spelling or held a child's hand in the schoolyard, there was always the wall of respect, apartness. You would never reach out to hug her impulsively. You might get her "holy habit" dirty or, even worse, disarrange the "cardboard" that held her veil in place.

She wondered why all the sisters had men's names instead of women's. Sister John the Baptist, Sister May Joseph, Sister

Albertus Magnus. And the orders they belonged to—Franciscans, Dominicans, Sisters of St. Joseph—had men's names, too.

Sitting in that church pew, growing up, she noticed other things. Though the nuns were dressed like the saints, like the women in the statues, they still weren't holy enough to be on the altar with men. But the men on the altar were dressed like women! They wore long, billowing robes and capes embroidered in gold and silver when they said Mass and prepared and served the Last Supper.

But if there were only men on the altar and in the processions, why did they talk about themselves as "holy Mother Church"? And how could a church be a "mother" if women were invisible?

There was, of course, the Blessed Mother. Her statues always radiated sweetness and encouragement. She was always young and pink-cheeked and slender, with hair cascading down to her waist. She was never shown to have a gray hair or a wrinkle, not even when she held her adult son across her lap in Michelangelo's *Pieta*. She seemed like some kind of fairy-tale princess, shimmering and awesome—not like a mother. The girl never would have thought to call *her* mother such names as Tower of Ivory, House of Gold, Star of the Sea, as they did in Mary's litany. Nor would she have described *any* woman she knew as the neighborhood women did in the prayers they said in the Legion of Mary meetings: "Who is she that comes forth as the morning rising, fair as the moon, bright as the sun, terrible as an army set in battle array?"[2]

But the message was that Mary could be used as a secret go-between, a kind of heavenly power broker who could "fix things" and, in a literal sense, "get her way." This was an image the church not only cultivated but institutionalized. *Is this what it meant to be a woman, a mother?* the girl in the pew wondered. The messages were both mixed and unclear. How could Mary "get around" Jesus to do anything and still be the sweet, gentle handmaid of the Lord? How could Mary be Our Lady of Sorrows in one parish and Queen of Heaven in the parish next door? As the most important woman in Christianity, was she weak or was she strong? The young girl grew up never being sure.

As she matured, she became even more disturbed by the contradictions, especially when she tried to relate to Mary as her model of sexuality. "If Mary is the model of the Christian community, the one who 'represents' us, then I need to feel she's a warm, loving, flesh-and-blood person," the teenager complained to Sister after class one day. "To be like Mary, you have to be a virgin and a mother simultaneously. No matter what you do, you lose either way!"

> The very conditions that make the Virgin sublime are beyond the powers of women to fulfill unless they deny their sex. Accepting the virgin as an ideal of purity implicitly demands rejecting the ordinary female condition as impure. Accepting virginity as an ideal entails contempt for sex and motherhood, with the result that far from remaining a privileged state undertaken by a few women of vocation, virginity and sexual chastity become a general condition of sinlessness applicable to both the married and the unmarried.[3]

Was the image of Mary's virginity more important than that of her maternity? No one could seem to tell her, perhaps because the church has hedged the question for centuries. Rather, it has chosen to indulge in theological handwringing over such matters as whether, in the process of delivering the child Jesus, her hymen did or did not remain "intact."

Were she to engage in a scriptural search to find Mary, the young girl would find the record more confusing still.

In *Alone of All Her Sex*, Marina Warner traces the development of Mariology over the centuries. She begins by noting that "the amount of historical information about the Virgin is negligible. Her birth, death, appearance, and age are never mentioned. During Christ's ministry, she plays a small part, and when she does appear, the circumstances are perplexing and often slighting."[4]

The chronologically first-written scriptural reference to Mary occurs in Saint Paul's letter to the Galatians (4:4). We are introduced to her inauspiciously when, in order to drive home his point about Jesus' humanity, Paul tells his readers that Jesus was "made of a woman." She remains nameless.[5]

She is mentioned primarily in Mark and in Luke's account of Christ's infancy (now acknowledged by scholars to be written more than eighty years after the events described took place). Marina Warner notes that the "only time she is at the heart of the drama in the Bible is in Luke's beautiful verses."[6]

There are only two conversations between Mother and Son which are reported in the gospels: the incident in the temple at Jerusalem when Jesus was twelve years old and the wedding feast at Cana.[7] She is mentioned as being present at the foot of the cross (Jn 19:26-30) and among those who were in the "upper room" at Jerusalem, where the apostles prayed following Jesus' Ascension (Ac 1:14). Then she is not mentioned again.

> Of the four declared dogmas about the Virgin Mary, her divine motherhood, her virginity, her immaculate conception, and her assumption into heaven, only the first can be unequivocally traced to Scripture, where Mary of Nazareth is undoubtedly the mother of Jesus.[8]

And yet, on the basis of this threadbare legacy, the church has constructed a Mariology that is awesome in the extreme.[9] Is it because, as the Mother of God, she was seen to be "useful"? In a patriarchal church, was she portrayed, basically, as all women have been, not in terms of who she was as a person, but as who *men needed her to be for them?* Judging from the historical over-view of Mary, this would seem to be the case.

Marina Warner points out that, depending on the cultural, theological, and political situation, Mary was imaged variously as a Second Eve (in the infant church, the model for virgins and martyrs), as a bejeweled queen, Maria Regina, in the sixth cen-tury when:

> the regal role of Mary as the Mother of God-Emperor became a central and forceful symbol of power which could be and was used to reinforce the Church's authority on earth. However, the honor paid Mary as Queen redounded to the honor of Queens, to the exclusion of other women.[10]

But with each embellishment, each title, each glorification, Mary's humanity seems to have receded.

> Every facet of the Virgin had been systematically developed to diminish, not increase, her likeness to the female condi-tion. Her freedom from sex, painful delivery, age, death and all sin exalted her, automatically, above ordinary women and showed them as inferior.[11]

"Well," said the young girl in the pew, "was she or was she not *once a human being*, this pregnant woman who was to become the prototype mother of all mothers—this woman who, we are told, represents the community of believers before the throne of God?"

Where, then, is the flesh-and-blood Mary with whom women of all ages down through the centuries can iden-tify...the pregnant woman whose muscles ache and whose flesh swells with her precious burden? As Mary walked toward her day of delivery, did the calves of her legs strain with fatigue? Did she ever arch her back with the sudden pain of a pulled muscle? Were her nights endless as she shifted and turned in her bed longing to find some position which might be comfortable? Were her breasts tender as her body began to prepare her milk glands to provide instant nourishment for the hungry Child?

Why has her humanity been denied us? Why can't theologians realize that nothing could speak to us more eloquently of her compassion and understanding than to know that she, like all mothers, worried and wept and struggled with a pregnancy she did not understand and a child who would be even more misunderstood?

Mary Dorsey suggests that perhaps this might be another reason why we hear Mary referred to often as "Our Lady." We would be forced to regard her differently if we called her Our Woman. The connotations of "lady" do not serve Mary or us well, she suggests. A lady is polite, romantic, well-bred, and helpless. She may be charming and even beautiful, but her character lacks two aspects vital to Christian maturity: sexuality and accountability.[12]

The young girl in the pew could appreciate that. Were she to explore further, she would find that this glorification of Mary did not change until the thirteenth and fourteenth centuries when, with the advent of the Franciscans, Mary came to be imaged as the barefoot virgin, wedded suddenly and surprisingly to poverty and humility. The friars:

> remolded her to their revolutionary ideals. . . . The Virgin left her starry throne in the heavens and laid aside her robes, insignia and diadem (including, apparently, her human crown in Saragossa, Spain, which contained over a million diamonds[13]) to sit, cross-legged, on the bare earth like a peasant mother with her child.

As Simone de Beauvoir has written:

> For the first time in human history the mother kneels before her son; she freely accepts her inferiority. This is the supreme

masculine victory, consummated in the cult of the Virgin—it is the rehabilitation of woman through the accomplishment of her defeat.[14]

From this point onward, Mary's cult of humility became institutionalized and has remained so down through the ages. It was not until 1974, in the papal encyclical *Marialis Cultis*, that Mary was imaged again culturally as the model of the "liberated woman."[15] Then it was acceptable for Mary, and therefore for all women, to finally get up off their knees.

But after so many centuries, women have forgotten how. Like the plaster statues with which they were surrounded in their childhoods, they are molded in a certain image. To break out of that image means to shatter the mold.

One of the strongest messages for a Catholic woman to overcome is the one that reminds her that she is born to suffer. As a daughter of Eve, she is not to be trusted. She must, because of Eve's action, "atone" for woman's sin. Our Lady of Sorrows as reflected in the sorrowful mysteries of the rosary is imaged in artwork by Mary's breast pierced with seven swords. Motherhood, not fatherhood, implies automatic suffering. So in imitation of Mary, millions of women yield in body, mind, and spirit to anguish they feel is holy, predictable, and natural. By programming them for suffering, the church maintains total control over their lives.

The result is what Anne Morrow Lindbergh quotes as *zerissenheit*, "torn-apartness."[16] The girl in the pew had only to reflect on the women in her own family to recognize that scenario unfolding day by day.

Thus Mary, the central woman in Christianity, was not only a model of suffering (as established by men) but a victim of suffering (as woman). As woman, not even she escaped manipulation by the church. The human qualities of docility and long-suffering which she exemplifies as a woman were extolled, unceasingly, by the church. What did this say to the girl in the pew about what it meant to be a woman, a wife, a mother? And because the church preached this image of women, wasn't this message reinforced by the girl's "good Catholic family"? Are these the kinds of human qualities we would inspire in young people, be they male or female, as potential leaders of the Christian community?

Patricia Noone points out that it is unfortunate that the symbol of the Virgin has often been used by the church to undermine, not to strengthen, the female self. Mary's power did not lead to the empowerment of others but simply to the preservation of the status quo.[17]

If the girl had taken a poll of her classmates of the second most popular woman in Catholicism, no doubt Mary Magdalene would have led the way. But mention of her was always cloudy. She was, after all, a sinner, a reformed prostitute. She was never a symbol of a woman who had suffered and wept and repented. She seemed important only because she symbolized God's generosity in forgiving her sins.

Elizabeth Schüssler Fiorenza points out that somehow, in all the sermons, Mary Magdalene was never imaged as the "apostle to the apostles"; that is, the woman so loved by Jesus, as a person, that he commissioned her, rather than the apostles, to spread the news of his resurrection to the world. This distortion of Mary Magdalene's image signals a deep distortion of the self-understanding of Christian women. Fiorenza notes that, even today, the women "said nothing to anyone, for they were afraid" (Mk 16:8).[18]

Had the young girl in the pew persisted, she might have tried the lives of the saints as another avenue for exploration. If so, what kind of women would she find who were thought to be "worthy" enough to be lifted out of anonymity? Who were the other women who were chosen to stand beside luminaries like Saint Teresa of Avila, Saint Joan of Arc, Saint Catherine of Siena, for example? Who were the choices of models for women to emulate down through the centuries? Over and over the message was clear: virgins and widows; sanctity without sex. The church reinforced its message. And when the church did choose to officially honor married women, wives and mothers, the message was essentially the same.

Doris Donnelly reminds us that the perplexing behavior and unusual styles of spirituality of married women like Jane Frances de Chantal, Catherine of Genoa, Bridget of Sweden, and Elizabeth of Hungary are cases in point: "Each one is honored not for her life as wife and mother but rather for the celibacy that she accepted after marriage, which included leaving children behind. . . ." as did Jane Frances de Chantal, in order to go out and form religious communities as part of her invitation to sanctity.[19]

Even in the case of Mother Elizabeth Seton, it was as a widow that she founded the Sisters of Charity and laid the foundation of the American Catholic parochial school system, events which undoubtedly contributed to her canonization in 1975 by Pope Paul VI. And although she reared and educated her children in the midst of this apostolic activity, she nevertheless remained a widow until her death.

"The church's recognition of these women would seem to confirm the notion that husbands and children in the flesh are an encumbrance, if not an insurmountable obstacle, of a life union with God."[20]

The mother of the girl in the pew might well ask how the church reconciled that message with a parallel one it promoted unceasingly: that it is in fidelity to our marriage vows, reflected in the cherishing of spouse and children, that we dignify the sanctity of matrimony.

She might also ask what constituted the essential difference between "abandoning" a husband in a loveless marriage (through divorce or separation) and abandoning a husband and family in order to pursue a "loftier" ideal of building religious communities.

In many ways, it would be easy for the girl in the pew to shrug off these women models as historical curiosities and to decide that somehow the church has "outgrown" such feminine imagery. If so, who could it offer her as replacements, as contemporary models for her time?

In 1950, Pope Pius XII canonized an eleven-year-old girl named Maria Goretti, a scant fifty years following her death. Her qualifications for martyrdom rested on the fact that she forfeited her life rather than lose her virginity. When a young man of her acquaintance attempted to rape her, she resisted and was brutally stabbed rather than submit to him. She forgave him freely on her deathbed and died the following day.

The church had not altered its message about the value of absolute virginity, even in the mid-twentieth century. Virginity and martyrdom continued to go hand in hand. Was the idea of losing one's life rather than losing one's virginity something that parents could feel comfortable teaching their daughters in the fifties? Is it something the church would be willing to witness to in hospitals and prisons and in today's rape centers to women who have been assaulted and have survived? One wonders if the church hears itself proclaiming that purity is more precious than life, on the one hand, while it mounts national campaigns to support right-to-life on the other. Women in families are certainly hearing the double message; and besides the mothers and daughters, the husbands and fathers and sons who love them are hearing it, too.

The girl who grew up in that pew in the fifties has daughters of her own now. Were she to find herself back in that pew, she need only glance at the immovable, pink-cheeked, plaster statues to know how much she has changed. Sitting there, as an adult, she can reflect on what her actual history in the church has been.

From Eve onward, the scenario was set. The first appearance of woman in the creation story showed her to be willful, disobedient, a trouble-maker. She has been feared and punished ever since. As civilizations heaved and sighed over the centuries, men continued to mistrust her and seemed obsessed with her body. Would it once again weaken them, seduce them, humiliate them (as Eve's did)?

Would it, on the other hand, provide them with the offspring they needed to plow their fields and fill their churches? Would it honor them with sons, with priests, to swell their patriarchal pride?

When women threatened them with their brains, as did the powerful abbesses in the Middle Ages, churchmen did not rest until they had essentially locked them in cloistered convents, where they were gradually "relieved" of any power they might once have enjoyed. In polite Victorian society, men's response to women was more subtle. The Victorian man kept women at arm's length by placing them upon a pedestal. It was safer and easier to keep them idealized.

In our time, the fear has become more difficult to deal with, perhaps because men now have to deal with the consequences of women's sophisticated sexuality. Now they must theologize about birth control, abortion, masturbation, artificial insemination while women act out the consequences of these decisions in terms of their minds and bodies. And since, more often than not, men's theology disregards women's reality, women end up, once again, as the losers, weighed down by a veritable laundry list of guilt.

Sitting in that pew after so long, the woman's eyes come to rest on the flickering lights of the votive candles. The hurricanes that have swept through the church in the last twenty years have not managed to dim them, somehow. She knows only, with a sudden loneliness, that *she* is different; the candleglow she sees no longer warms her or leads her. She has changed.

The women she looked to once can no longer give her answers that will soothe her. They would not know how to claim her questions as their own. The rustling skirts of the starched, scrubbed nuns have vanished. She cannot commend the virgin martyrs to her daughters. She cannot even relate to them herself.

There is, deep down within her, a longing for the Blessed Mother Mary (not the Virgin). She feels, somehow, that she lost her long before she found her. Now that her own mother is gone, she needs Mary more than she ever knew.

But she knows now that she is, has been, will be alone, essentially. And yet, because of this, she is no longer afraid. Knowing that she is her only dependent, she knows, too, that only she has the power to love herself enough to say yes or no to the world outside.

Then what is she doing here in this church of her childhood? What does she hope to find in this place she knows she has long outgrown?

"God is the country of the spirit," wrote Dylan Thomas. "Each of us is given a little holding of ground in that country."[21]

She has come, she realizes, to stake a claim for herself in that country. Having survived her history as a Catholic woman, she has come to claim her inheritance as a Christian.

Faith, she has learned, can be harvested in many ways.

CHAPTER FIVE

Women and Men

Is Human Liberation Possible?

"In our life in the Lord . . . woman is not independent of man, nor is man independent of woman. For as woman was made from man, in the same way man is born of woman." (I Co 11:11-12)

"Ironically, as more women are finding their identities, more men are losing theirs. Thus women must add one more role to their growing repertoire, that of guide . . . or at least fellow searcher. Together they may not find separate identities as man and woman, but a common identity as humans."[1]

Anthony Pietropinto and
Jacqueline Simenauer

THEY ARE, THEY TELL US, masked men. One sees them everywhere. They crowd the airports of every city, their attaché cases at their sides like extended limbs, their brains rectangularized in expensive leather. They sit behind the wheels of trucks and taxi cabs and Cadillacs, each of them twins since they are both the drivers and the driven. They hold the reins. They are in charge, responsible, in control. Every message they receive tells them they can be, should be, must be Mr. Success. They populate the playing fields, caught up in corporate games that sweep through union halls and universities and Little Leagues alike, infecting men with winner's fever, a sickness that stalks them even in bed.

Winning is everything. But since we know that somewhere, sometime, someone has to lose, the men invariably become statistics. Slowly, surely, they succumb, victims of psychic exhaustion—a disease that increasingly seems to be cured only by death.

And yet, they say, they cannot remove the masks; they dare not. But at least, now, they are beginning to ask themselves the reasons why. They watch as women struggle and succeed in transcending their limitations. They ask themselves what this will mean to them. They cannot ignore the sinking in their stomachs when a woman gets the job they had been working for.

They know their feelings, what they fear, what they stand to lose when they are forced to relate to women as competitors rather than comforters. Increasingly, they are turning inward with new kinds of questions about where they've come from, where they're going, where they are. They know that their answers are more a matter of survival than philosophy.

In his book, *The Hazards of Being Male*, psychologist Herb Goldberg outlines some of the messages men receive:

> From early childhood on, the boy learns that masculinity means not depending on anybody. . . . Dependency in the male mind spells disaster. . . . [Thus] the male heroes in our culture are the "untouchables," cold, self-contained and with no apparent need for such sissy behavior. . . . Feelings become unknown, unpredictable quantities, expressions of which threaten him and make him feel vulnerable. . . .
>
> Because feelings are not permitted free expression, the male lives in constant reaction against himself. What he is on the outside is a facade, a defense against what he really is on the inside. He controls himself by denying himself.[2]

Lawyer author Marc Feigen Fasteau agrees. "Men have carried the practice of emotional restraint to the point of paralysis," he says.[3]

Whether or not it is true that "men are more fragile than women," as one man suggested, the fact is that since the mask is, after all, invisible, most men will angrily deny it. They will label the male image as "good sportsmanship," "teamwork," "executive cool," "the American way."

They certainly will not discuss their fears or feelings of inadequacy in the locker room or at the board meeting. (It's bad enough to fail with women; it would be devastating to show their vulnerability to other men.) Some are able to share their burdens. Usually it is because there is a woman waiting somewhere, someplace at the end of the day.

Women know the mask well. They know its toll (on families, marriages, relationships); they know its price (upward mobility, moonlighting, relocation, traveling). It is these women who so often bear the emotional brunt of the mask's consequences as they stand by helplessly watching the effects of ulcers, coronaries, alcoholism.

Statistically they have been told that they will be widows for a minimum of eight years.[4] The fact is, that as a society, we are killing off our men. What is even more alarming is that this process begins so early. According to Goldberg, boys are seen in child-guidance clinics at a rate which is often three times as high as girls,[5] afflicted with autism (a form of childhood schizophrenia), dyslexia, and stuttering.[6]

At nearly every age level from birth to death, the male mortality rate is significantly higher, although the birthrate for men and women is almost the same.[7]

Men commit suicide three to four times more often than women.[8]

Men have a 40% higher rate of cancer[9] and a staggering 400% higher rate of heart disease.[10]

Men outnumber women by 50% in chronic disease hospitals.[11] The list goes on and on.

Enter the liberated woman.

I speak here not of the radical feminist with dazzling rhetoric and awesome personal and professional credentials. I refer, rather, to the wife and mother who one day went from super-volunteer to super sales-manager in a corporation, the girl friend who demands sexual satisfaction in an age of options, the daughter who sails through classes in auto mechanics and doesn't need Dad's advice on how to fix her car, the bride whose career provides far more excitement than the thought of pregnancy.

But that's just the home front.

Then there's the world of work.

If a man's an employer, he has different problems coping with women. There are the hassles with Equal Opportunity Employment, Affirmative Action, The Fair Employment Practice Commission, not to mention the problem of separate rest rooms and accommodations for women in "non-traditional" jobs.

On the line, men watch as one by one the "male" job market changes. By law, women are climbing telephone poles, working on oil rigs, racing at Indianapolis, conducting symphony orchestras, and flying commercial passenger jets. They have forever changed the elitist all-male image at West Point and Annapolis just as they have begun the process of liberating an all-male priesthood to one of shared responsibility.

In the area of the man's role as "head of the house," one has only to look at the status of the American family to see how precarious that position has become. Divorce, remarriage, and single parenthood have caught men off-balance. Their non-presence to their families, due to traveling on the job or moonlighting, causes them to further abdicate their responsibility as husbands and fathers. According to one study, there are four million working-class married men between the ages of twenty-five to forty who moonlight. This is happening at a time when their children need them most![12]

And even if a man and wife have struggled for years to raise a "good" family, increasingly, the man feels impotent as a father to his growing children, especially his teenagers. Often he watches in fear and frustration as the influence of drugs, alcohol, pregnancy, and abortion surround his family. Where once his word was "law," his "authority" is often hollow. Once again he is confronted with a sense of powerlessness and vulnerability.

He is hardly the image of the ideal man that his culture says he ought to be: the sleek, tuxedo-clad playboy in the car commercial surrounded by a covey of adoring blondes. Hardly the athlete whose body and brains command a six-figure salary, and certainly not the gunslinger whose courage and cunning always saved the day.

All of these are "real men" because they are in control.

> Having lost the sports arena, the military battleground and the job field as his proving grounds, today's man is left only with the bedroom as his testing site for his masculinity. Woman becomes his judge and his validator, as well as his conquest or companion. . . . Many men are therefore not just seeking reassurance that they are good sexual performers, but that they are men. . . . [13]

As a result, it is men who are in the majority in sex therapy clinics.[14] Competition does not, alas, encourage intimacy.

The realization that men in our culture are, statistically, in a far more critical situation than women only compounds the problem of human liberation. While men are slow to acknowledge it, at least outwardly, women have a different set of problems when confronted with the information.

Where men wear masks, women wear veils.

Although all will express concern, and many assume guilt for men's problems, many wives and mothers will claim that maintaining the current family status quo is difficult enough without pushing for additional demands on the husband/wife relationship. Many will say that they're already worn out trying to keep track of children, homes, part-time jobs, and, in the time that's left over, themselves, without initiating or even forcing new patterns of communications with their spouses. Many of them will add, almost as an afterthought, "Besides, I know it won't do any good because I've tried."

Some married women will greet the information with apathy. For a variety of reasons, they want to be left alone to pursue their own interests and to stay in what has essentially become a comfortable holding pattern. As "married singles," they maintain a semblance of unity with their partners to the outside world, but in actuality, they are nourished by their fantasy life more than by reality.

Single women, whether unmarried, divorced, or widowed, struggling to maintain their social and sexual equilibrium, report increasingly that they are discouraged in attempts to relate to men who seem either unwilling or unable to become involved in permanent relationships that include marriage and/or fidelity.

And while feminists, as a group, tend to be sensitive to men's problems simply because they so often encounter men's fear as the block in their own struggles, they have, they remind us, wept and bled for far too long to give up what they've gained.

There are, of course, countless women everywhere who are deeply caring and acutely aware of men's problems. They have and will continue to explore every possibility presented to them to work for healing, reconciliation, and growth in their relationships with men. But they are the first to acknowledge that they cannot do it alone.

Nor do they want to.

For if anything gives a feminist—any woman—pause, it is the realization that as women climb the corporate ladder, they begin acquiring men's medical histories, namely, symptoms spawned by stress, competition, and professional overload.

So women, too, now have a new set of questions.

Is the price, they ask, really commensurate with the reward? Will we both be so confused and exhausted in the scramble for sex-role superiority that we will become ciphers? *If a man's strength is predicated on a woman's weakness, then how strong is he?*

How long will it take us to realize that we are running out of alternatives? How many statistics will it take to call a truce to our fear and loneliness? Can't we see that, as women and men, we are both afraid of losing ground, taking risks, jeopardizing what we have come to regard as our "security"?

Is this why Jesus came? to make us less than human? with no hope of ever being free? Once again, we have only to look at who Jesus was: what he said, how he acted when he lived among us. No moment of his life was without meaning.

Jesus came to deliver us from bondage, to free us from ourselves. He came to release us from the prisons of fear and doubt, anxiety and loneliness. He came to give us the courage to take off our masks and veils. But he never asked anything of us without first showing us the way.

Jesus was a man. But by today's standards of maleness, Jesus was hardly in control. He would never have qualified for a Marlboro man commercial or provided the image of a tough-cop hero on television. He was never "cool," or "untouchable"—certainly not the model for Mr. Success. His vulnerability took him to a cross where he died, by all accounts, a loser, still proclaiming his dependence on a Father he should have, by then, long outgrown. He was a man totally in touch with his emotions; therefore he had everything to gain and nothing to lose.

Men should remember that Jesus was not afraid to cry. At Lazarus' death, we are told that when Jesus saw Mary and the Jews weeping, "he was troubled in spirit and moved by the deepest emotions"! And when he saw Lazarus, "Jesus wept," which caused the Jews to say, "See how much he loved him"(Jn 11:33-36).

Men should be aware that Jesus was not afraid to show his fear. In Gethsemane with his disciples, we are told that "grief and anguish came over him and he said to them, 'The sorrow in my heart is so great that it almost crushes me. Stay here and watch with me' " (Mk 14:34). And later, "In great anguish, he prayed even more fervently, his sweat was like drops of blood falling to the ground" (Lk 22:44). Men should recall that Jesus was not afraid to accept help from women.

> . . .Jesus traveled through towns and villages preaching the Good News. . . . The twelve disciples went with him, and so did some women. . . . Mary Magdalene . . . Joanna . . . and Susanna, and many other women who used their own resources to help Jesus and his disciples (Lk 8:1-3).

Men should take courage knowing that Jesus was not afraid to show tenderness. He even chose to use a feminine maternal image. "Jerusalem, Jerusalem! you kill the prophets, you stone the messengers God has sent you! How many times I wanted to put my arms around all your people, just as a hen gathers her chicks under her wings!" (Lk 13:34).

But perhaps most awesome of all was Jesus' ability to completely surrender to the force of faith, even when he could not see its source in a crowd of strangers. We read simply, "Jesus said, 'Someone touched me for I knew it when power went out of me!' " The woman came, trembling, and threw herself at Jesus' feet. Jesus said to her, "My daughter, your faith has made you well. Go in peace!" (Lk 8:46-48).

Peace. How easily we say it, long for it, beg for it: the peace that passes all understanding; the peace that we can only give to others when we have, perhaps through the miracle of a single moment, experienced it ourselves. But we cannot give what we do not have.

So perhaps the first step in the struggle of the masks and the veils is to pray for the courage to give, to share what we *do* have, even if we wish that it were something better, something more.

Maybe we have forgotten that we alone have the keys to the kingdom, but that others cannot hear us unless we let them in.

Perhaps the most precious thing we have to share with strangers—with husbands, lovers, wives, children, parents, friends—is our fear, indeed our terror, of the dark, our insecurities, our guilt. We might, then, proceed to unlock still more doors along the corridor—our fear of failure, of appearing foolish, of always saying too much or not enough, the thousand games we play in order just to stay alive.

With a little more courage, we might explore our secret capacity for punishing not only others but ourselves as well. (Sooner or later we all qualify for punishment because we are at some time either too young, too old, too sick, too rich, too tired, too poor, too dark, too light, too weak, too strong. The list goes on and on.)

What a relief it will be to all of us to find out, in the sharing, that we all have the same secrets: that we are not alone; that there is, because of him, a holiness in being human, a holiness in tears and fear, and dependency and tenderness; that, by surrendering in faith, we, too, as *friends,* can call the power out of Him.

A closed fist may be protected, but it also is unable both to give and to receive. Only by opening it up and stretching forth our hands, palms open, can we become gift-givers, Christians.

For far too long, each of us has been a solitary porter, struggling, often in desperation, under the deadweight luggage of our fears. It is time to begin to trust our fellow travelers, knowing that it is human to stop by the side of the road to rest and share with one another for a while.

Jesus traveled light. He had with him everything he needed. So do we. It is something to remember the next time we think we should outguess, outwit, outreach our neighbors. It is a game played only by masked men and veiled women who, in reality, are really only hiding from themselves.

For Every Woman

For every woman who is tired of acting weak
    when she knows she is strong,
There is a man who is tired of appearing strong
    when he feels vulnerable;

For every woman who is tired of acting dumb,
There is a man who is burdened
    with the constant expectation of "knowing everything";

For every woman who is tired of being called
    "an emotional female,"
There is a man who is denied the right to weep
    and to be gentle;

For every woman who is called unfeminine
    when she competes,
There is a man for whom competition is the only way
    to prove his masculinity;

For every woman who is tired of being a sex object,
There is a man who must worry about his potency;

For every woman who feels "tied down" by her children,
There is a man who is denied the full pleasures
    of shared parenthood;

For every woman who is denied meaningful employment
    or equal pay,
There is a man who must bear full financial responsibility
    for another human being;

For every woman who was not taught the intricacies
    of an automobile,
There is a man who was not taught
    the satisfaction of cooking;

For every woman who takes a step toward her own
    liberation,
There is a man who finds the way to freedom
    has been made a little easier.[1]

Nancy R. Smith

CHAPTER SIX

Who Are the Women in the Church?
And What Do They Need from Each Other?

*"Let's not wait to tell other women how beautiful they are. Let's
let them know that their dedication and generosity as single women,
as wives and mothers has been and continues to be a source of hope to
us . . . that their efforts to make something of a difficult job, as well
as to work at their marriage relationships has given us the courage
to begin again, to renew our commitments. Let us be to one another
challenge, joy, hope, support."*[1]

Sister Lisa Marie Lazio, OP

SISTER DANIELLE GOMEZ, OFS,
is asked to give a house blessing. She makes an appointment
beforehand and goes to the home to meet the family. With
them, she goes from room to room asking questions gently:
Who lives in each of the rooms? What are they used for? What
important things happen there? They also ask her to bless their
pickup truck. Again, she asks how the family uses it: Where does
it go? What does it do? How does it help the family?

When she returns, her blessing incorporates all the words
and feelings the family has shared with her. The blessing
becomes a meditation, a prayer of thanksgiving and a celebration for the family. As a woman, she has brought a special
dimension of sensitivity to her ministry because she has drawn
on her life experience.

• Two women sit in a restaurant patio in the California sun-
shine. They are both well-dressed, attractive, in their forties.

Passing strangers glance a second time at one of the women, a fragile blonde who is speaking softly, but with great feeling. She is telling her friend, a married woman of twenty-five years, her story. It is the story of her love affair with a married man. She is a nun.

She has traveled across the country to talk with this woman.

"You're the only one I could trust to be honest with me. I was desperate because only someone in your position can give me perspective. I need you to give me the courage to leave him by helping me understand what it must be like for his wife and family."

• Sister Patrice Underwood, IHM, ministers at the bedside of a woman who has just undergone a double mastectomy. She holds the woman's hand as she speaks.

Together they reflect on just what has happened in terms of both the woman's body and spirit. She helps the woman talk about what her breasts had meant to her: the nourishment they had given her children; the feeling of femininity and attractiveness they had contributed to her pride in her body; the pleasure they had provided her and her husband in love-making. Together, as women, they mourn the loss. With women's words, they pray.

Women helping women.

This is not nuns helping housewives, nor mothers helping sisters, nor women religious helping religious women.

This is *women* helping *women*.

We have done it always—intuitively, spontaneously, creatively; as we problem-solved over coffee in suburbia; when we counseled in the classroom or held a hand at a hospital bedside; when we brought in food for families after funerals; when we simply sat at the other end of a telephone and listened to the sounds of a breaking heart.

We have done it most eloquently when we have been ourselves. But we have never given it a name. We have never seen it as ministry, a ministry to women, our ministry to one another.

Maybe it's because, as women, we were taught that ministry was something only a man was qualified to "do" to others. Maybe it's because we were socialized into thinking that if a woman needed help (ministering to), it was because she couldn't cope. Maybe it's because our cries for help were interpreted as liabilities ("Women are so emotional!"), and so we hastened to trivialize them or dismiss them. Maybe it's because we were taught that only by living for others were we truly ever able to achieve happiness. Maybe just admitting that we had needs made us feel inadequate and ashamed.

It is not difficult to see that if we thought our problems were unimportant, then we were unimportant. It was easy to sweep our needs and fears and dreams under the umbrella of "girl talk." We never acknowledged the fact that, as women, we were life-savers for one another, much less *life-givers*. Whenever women met to share, it was spoken of as a "hen party" or a "gab session," a kind of joke.

With some variations, it is a history shared by both laywomen and women religious. But because we have never shared our lives, our stories, our needs as women, we have related to each other in terms of our separate life-styles. We have focused, usually defensively, on how we differ rather than on what we share.

Consequently, through a lack of communication, we have been denied access to one another and thereby have become divided against each other, which has led to a host of myths and misconceptions about each other as persons. It is as though we had forgotten that we walk around in the same bodies, share the same conditioning in the church and society, share the same memories of what it means to be a woman growing up in a family.

As nuns and laywomen looked at each other across the pews at Sunday Mass, what were their thoughts of one another? When their eyes rested on a favorite child they had in class, surrounded now by a family who alternately hugged and quieted him during the long sermon, what did the nuns think?

They knew from their own memories that for a mother, family life was often upside-down, grey-tired, and full of left-overs and loose ends.

Yet for one nun, Sister Eileen, behind the smile there was the aching awareness that that squirming child was the *woman's* child (not on loan for school days). She knew, too, that the home to which this mother would return was probably not scrubbed and polished (like the convent), but it was *her* home (not the property of the community). It included schedules which occasionally stretched to include unswept floors and unmade beds and children's birthday parties, where ice cream and cake invariably were ground into the rug. It was home where there was no bell to begin and end the day, no unswerving consideration of the common rule, the common good, the common room (where one was expected to share cheerfully in the recreation); a home where permission was not needed, at every turn, to write a letter, plant a garden, take an aspirin.

Sister Patricia, sitting next to her, would also be smiling, but her smile would mean something altogether different. She would look at the same child with love, but her feelings came from another source. "I was self-satisfied. I never had feelings to contradict that. I never resented what other women, especially mothers, had because I knew I was better than they were. I was married to Jesus, and the children in the classroom were the children of that marriage.

"My relationship with these women consisted of role-to-role relationships. I was the teacher relating to the parent. They were mothers, never persons. After all those years, I recall only one woman, but I never called her by name. I never called her Mary Maguire. She was only Johnny Maguire's mother.

"I never knew I had a body, I never felt I had anything under those layers of clothing. But then, you weren't supposed to have a body. You were only supposed to have a soul.

"It was only later on that I began to realize that the reason I couldn't relate to laywomen was that I felt less than a woman myself, less, in fact, than laywomen. For that reason, also, I never felt I would be attractive to men.

"Gradually, I began to realize that when laywomen talked to me, trusted me, shared their stories with me, they considered me one of them.

"I began to see that for years women, for me, were essentially strangers, and that if we were ever going to get together, then we had to set about ways of healing one another."

And so they sat, smiling at each other across the pews, carefully separate, unaware of how deeply they shared in one another's destiny. Certainly they shared similar beginnings in a family, and therefore nuns knew far more about the daily lives of laywomen than laywomen knew about what went on behind convent walls.

As they drove off with their contingent of youngsters, how many car-pool mothers would call out to their children's teachers, "Oh, you're so lucky to be able to retreat to your clean, peaceful convent and have all that quiet time to pray!" And at Sunday Mass, these same mothers, struggling now with their squirming children, would sigh again momentarily as they caught sight of the serene profiles of the sisters as they sat together in prayer, filling the first few pews nearest the altar. In their silence, they looked like some remote and awesome still life from another century. The mothers thought, *No clutter, no confusion, no measles and unpaid bills and sticky jam along the kitchen woodwork. Only the soft demands of moving to the rhythms of fully balanced days filled with inspiring work and unhurried prayer.*

Nothing in the older nuns' gentle reserve suggested the price they had paid for that quiet space and "freedom." They never spoke about the fabric of their early formation in the novitiate. For many, entrance into religious life meant personal obliteration: a new name (usually a man's name) and, in some cases, a number; having one's hair cropped and one's body hidden beneath asexual clothing (which, for some, included seven layers of linen and some cardboard around the neck and head linen requiring thirty-three pins to keep it in place).

It meant surrendering one's will as well as one's identity: One was to view nature and the world as "evil," an attitude which included "forgetting" one's family, being forbidden to hold or carry a baby, and being on constant guard against temptation by keeping strict "custody of the eyes."

Human support, even among one's own living community, was forbidden, under the dire warning to avoid "particular friendships." Having been called and somehow miraculously "chosen," they should not depend on people. They were nuns now. God was enough.

Spirituality was "encouraged" by the public recitation of each member's infractions of the rules before the entire community at a public confessional known as the Chapter of Faults. (One nun reported that if she couldn't think of anything, she invented something—even if it meant deliberately breaking a dish—so she'd have something to confess.) Privately, one was instructed to pray for and actively seek humiliations, which, for some, included the mindless, self-abasing daily act of kissing the floor.

In some communities, sisters were required to kneel before superiors when asking permission for personal hygiene articles. One sister reported that they were refused sanitary napkins in her community because, they were told, they were too "worldly." Instead, they had to wear "rags" for which they were personally responsible. This meant laundering and hanging them out on the clothesline "only at night."

Perhaps one of the most dramatic examples of adjustment for a woman entering religious life was the report of one former nun who stated that shortly after entering her community, her menstrual period ceased, for no discernable physiological reason. "I think my body received the message that I was now neutered," she said. "Consequently, all my female systems shut down." Years later, after leaving religious life, again for no apparent medical reason, her menstrual cycle resumed.

"They trained us well, and like good children, we were good students," said former Sister John Michael. "The only trouble was that even though our growth was somewhat stunted, some of us still managed to grow up."

How ironic that the founders of many of these religious congregations were themselves brilliant, aggressive, self-actualized women who were, by necessity, highly motivated and strong-willed in pursuit of their goals to build the kingdom. Were they alive today, they might find that among the very people whose needs they were inspired to respond to—the neglected, the deprived, the suffering—might well be the religious women who comprise the communities which bear their names.

But though the journeys of laywomen and women religious differ in detail, they are parallel in consequence. Both groups warred against their bodies, seeing them as an enemy to be defeated. Both struggled for breathing space in the Spirit, for the strength to "offer up" their suffering without a murmur. At the same time, they were charged with responsibility for both instilling the faith and inspiring a "burning love for God" in the children in their classrooms and families.

It was the women whose example was supposed to provide vocations for "good Catholic schools" and "good Catholic homes." It was the nuns who were responsible for nurturing interest in the classroom for their young charges to become altar boys; it was the mother's responsibility to rouse their sleepy young sons up to serve Mass on those cold winter mornings. It was mother's responsibility if the children didn't do their home-work, while Sister felt somehow "responsible" if Johnny didn't "pass."

Yet both knew, without ever questioning it, that no starched nun's habit or mother's annual pregnancy would ever promote her status in the church beyond that of servant. With few varia-tions, their lives would be orchestrated by men.

They may have worked side by side for weeks, months, or even years on parish projects (raising money to build schools and gymnasia, to enlarge cafeterias, to furnish convents, to staff CCDs), yet it never occurred to them to sit down together and discuss how they might share the responsibility of deciding how that money should be spent! It seems all the more incredible when one considers the qualifications of these women: many of them were heads of households and principals of large parish schools. Without question, they did the work, raised the money, and turned the check over to the pastor. After all, "Father knew best."

And while laywomen were busy juggling bake sales, driving car-pools, and organizing rummage sales, women religious were struggling under burdens of their own. Restricted on every side by rules which reduced them to child-like dependency in matters of communication, travel, and interpersonal relationships, nuns were subjected to still another agenda: education. It was on-going, unrelenting, and entirely predictable. Since part of the rationale of religious communities was to keep the sisters pro-ductive (i.e., busy) from dawn to dusk (so, as one sister noted, they wouldn't have time to "get into trouble") hardly had the last blackboard been washed in the classroom when the sisters were off to summer school. Education as a priority is reflected in a statistic which shows that in one congregation alone, ninety percent of the members under forty in one community of 1600 hold master's degrees. The other ten percent are working on the higher degree.[2]

But if, indeed, they had the "leisure" to study, read, pray, and attend yet another session of summer school, then why weren't they given the opportunity to share the fruits of their study and meditation, at least with other women outside the convent walls? For whom were they being educated—for themselves and their equally educated communities—or for the People of God?

How many nuns have lamented that, following Vatican II, they longed to share their new knowledge and insights from such documents as the *Church in the Modern World* and the *Decree on the Apostolate of the Laity* with the very people for whom these words were intended, and who so desperately needed to hear them? Called to a new vision, a new set of possibilities for the People of God, they felt frustrated that there was neither the time nor the opportunity to do so for almost a decade. By that time, tens of thousands of women, mostly in their twenties and thirties, had left religious life.

Among them was Alabaman Mary Hendrick. For her, making that decision to leave represented "the first time, as a Catholic woman, that I felt I had control of my life. I knew, without a shadow of a doubt, that I was free to live out my own life and that I had every right to make that choice."

That sense of freedom has become, since Vatican II, the hallmark of Christian women throughout the church today. In increasing numbers, they are echoing the words of scripture which proclaim, "Am I not free? Am I not an apostle?" (1 Cor. 9:1—Douay) and "Christ has set us free! Stand, then, as free people, and do not allow yourselves to become slaves again" (Ga 5:1).

It is a message that Sister Martha Tomas of Chicago's Loyola University feels is the most precious gift she can share with women today. "I would like her to know a whole new revelation about Christ, a whole new element that makes us free! When Christ liberated us, He did not place limitations on our expectations of 'freedom in the Lord.' He wants me to be free enough to pray, to look at myself and free myself of my own self-limiting images. He wants me to be free enough to love people in my own way."

Essential to that need for freedom is the need women have to be taken seriously as human beings, much less Christians. Where is justice, they ask, in a church which "allows" women to labor but not to vote? The church's continuing refusal to implement its own teachings perpetuates its reputation for giving lie to its own pronouncements. It has been over a decade since the Vatican II Council fathers proclaimed, "While the church is bound to give witness to justice, she recognizes that anyone who ventures to speak to the people about justice must first be just in their eyes."[3]

Even today, despite the fact that women religious have publicly taken vows which include the forfeiture of marriage, family, and material property, they nevertheless retain the same status as laywomen. For both, only six of the seven sacraments are available to them as "laywomen." Only men are regarded as worthy enough to qualify for all the sacraments—the seventh being the sacrament of Holy Orders.

Historically, because all women's energy was directed toward making themselves acceptable to men (father, husband, boss, priest), they never looked at other women's opinions as being of significance. Consequently, they never looked to other women to affirm and support them. Because they never listened to or trusted their own voices, they never really heard the voices of other women as being ultimately important or significant.

Often women resist liberation because we have been taught that our bodies are weaker, our powers of reasoning defective, our intellects lighter, our skills inferior, our emotions frivolous. And we have believed our teachers. We suffer from low self-esteem and no self-confidence. Women's liberation has been termed an "identity crisis." Women are beginning to ask "Who am I? What does it mean to say that *I* have been created in the image of God?" Christ commanded us to love others as we love ourselves, but we women have been taught to despise ourselves.

And so we have mistrusted other women. We prefer a man to cut our hair, carve our meat, service our car, preach us a sermon. We say we wouldn't work for a woman executive or vote for a woman president. We really do believe that we and all other women are inferior to men. Men sometimes see other men as a part of the "team" but women usually view each other as "competition." It's time we began practicing sisterhood as well as brotherhood.[4]

Perhaps a good place to begin would be to start examining some of the myths which have kept us separate. Sister Joan Doyle, PBVM, sees the question of celibacy as one which has the potential of dividing Catholic women.

Celibacy

"Celibacy is not necessarily a 'better way to live your life,' " insists Sister Joan. "But for centuries our life-style was held up to be 'better.' That very life-style restricted us from dialoguing with laywomen. Only since Vatican II have we been removed from our isolated pedestal. The ancient chasm will be difficult to bridge." But she is hopeful, noting that everywhere "women are trying to reach out to each other in reconciliation and healing."[5]

Laywomen and women religious might begin by taking the time to discuss what their common understanding of celibacy actually is. Is celibacy simply abstinence from genital relations?

Does it exclude relationships which encourage dependency or foster intimacy? Does it preclude making oneself vulnerable to others in high risk situations, either socially or on the job?

Limiting the discussion solely to genital relations, laywomen and women religious may be surprised to discover how much they have in common as women. Countless numbers of women, both single and married, choose to spend great portions of their lives in non-genital activity, either because of life-style or medical necessity.

Certainly women who have chosen to use natural family planning can attest to the fact that a conscious choice for genital abstinence must be made almost daily while one is relating intimately with a partner or spouse. And what of the thousands of single women who have chosen not to marry and/or have genital relationships, as well as women who are widowed, separated, or divorced?

What new understandings can we share with one another that will help in our mutual healing of ourselves and one another?

As women—celibate, single, married, divorced, and widowed—what has been our experience of celibacy?

In terms of both a temporary and lifelong commitment, how have we coped with it?

Has it been a gift or a burden?

What effect has it had on our bodies and spirits; indeed, on the totality of our lives?

Again, in terms of our life experience, what correlations can we make between celibacy and chastity? Where, if at all, do they intersect?

Drawing on our feminine life experience, perhaps we, as women, need to begin forming new definitions, not only of celibacy, but also of chastity. What does it mean for a woman, both as person and as partner, to be single-hearted in her love for her Lord?

What insights can we share with one another that will help us to understand the women whom we encounter in our ministries? How can we draw on, learn from, and integrate the work of contemporary behavioral scientists and theologians? Together, what can we learn about what it means to be whole, to be human, to grow in the Lord?

Dutch psychologist Father Henri Nouwen, in a speech at Rome's North American College, stated that all Christians, not just priests and religious, are called to lead a celibate life. Nouwen said that celibacy, understood as leaving a "vacancy for God" in life, is a vocation even for married Christians.

"Celibacy is part of marriage," he said, "because the intimacy of marriage is based on participation in a love that is greater than the love which the couple can offer each other." He went on to say that even for priests and religious sexual abstinence "can never be the most important part of celibacy."

Further, he opposed the traditional view of defending celibacy for its "usefulness," that is, as a tool for keeping a person's time and energies free for others. For Father Nouwen, the true celibate "recognizes God's ultimate priority by being useless in his presence," by standing "naked, powerless and vulnerable before God. . . . Making celibacy 'useful'," he said, "is more a homage to American pragmatism" than the acceptance of celibacy for God.

"Celibacy is an openness to God, lived in a way that must raise questions to those we encounter about the deeper meaning of existence." He warned priests and religious about viewing celibacy as an "elitist" vocation intended for only a few. Celibacy should be seen as a charism of openness to which all Christians are called rather than just another elitist barrier separating religious from the people they were ordained to serve.[6]

Elitism

"The sisters? We thought they were saints," said Californian Jody Teichner. "Even in the classroom, we never doubted they were perfect. No matter what they said or did, there was no way for a sister to be wrong."

Annalise Haas's memories of nuns are part of a warm, secure childhood in New Jersey. All through grade school and high school, they were her teachers. But today when she recalls them, she does not refer to them in the way she speaks of other women. "We all knew that nuns weren't human!" she says with a mischievous grin that turns into a chuckle. "Nuns were . . . well . . . they just weren't *like* us. Somehow, they were always way up there!"

"It was one of those things we all accepted without question," says Joan Clancy of her Catholic girlhood in Boston. "If a girl became a nun, it was because she was somehow better than we were. She had to be or she wouldn't have had a vocation. It was the signal that you were holier, kinder, more 'religious' than the rest of us.

"Outwardly, we shrugged it off, but down deep we always felt we never made the grade, that we weren't 'good enough.'

"The so-called cream-of-the-crop went into religious life. The leftovers, like us, got married and had a bunch of kids."

What does it mean to be better, to be different, to be special? What has it cost the church to put a price tag on a group of individuals which guarantees that they are "perfect," that they are "always right," that they can never fail? Does it mean that they are closer to Christ because they have the advantage in love or sacrifice? Or does it mean that they simply don't need the things that other women need?

To be "set apart" as women religious have been traditionally, says, in the deepest sense, that nuns are not human: that they never fall in love, never get pregnant, never masturbate, never get abortions; that they are never alcoholic, incompetent, emotionally disturbed, drug-addicted, *human*; that they are not part of the gay community which comprises ten percent of the nation's population; that they have somehow transcended the normal needs of their bodies and hence the consequences of menstruation, physical desire, menopause.

And so, with this script, what are the options open to these women? Are they to live the lives of religious automatons to satisfy *our* need for the presence of perfection among us? Does knowing that they witness so profoundly absolve us from our responsibility to do likewise? Knowing that they give visible example by their lives as Christians, do we feel a little less accountable, a little less under pressure, a little less "on the line"?

Or do nuns risk our discomfort and possible rejection of them by their living, working, and dressing as we do and letting their actions witness to who they are and what they are about?

Together, laywomen and women religious must sit down and talk about the areas in their respective lives where each of them is loneliest, most frustrated, most afraid. Simply put, we must allow ourselves to be vulnerable, to trust enough to be able to say to one another, "I will show you what I have in my pocket so you will have the courage to show me what you have in yours."

How have the messages each of us have received from the church affected our life decisions, our personal and professional relationships, our bodies, our souls? With patience and prayer, this sharing can be, ultimately, only a relief, a "freeing up" of impossible and unnecessary burdens which have been carried, like crushing backpacks, on our individual shoulders for years. Together, we can discard the assumptions, the myths, the expectations, the misunderstandings, the anger—all the cobwebs which develop when people are not allowed to reach out to one another. No matter how subtle the separation, it is discrimination in its most divisive form.

Woman's capacity for prayer and hospitality, traditionally at the service of men in the church, must now be directed towards the needs of women. The time has come for women in the church to take responsibility for their lives and for the lives of other women. For, as Helen Pyne reminds us, if we persist in ignoring the problems of others, we only continue to protect their discontent.

It has been said that protection from participation is a deprivation of rights. But for those who minister, I believe it is far more. To foster separation, thereby precluding access to areas of communication concerning human suffering, is for Christians both a scandal and a tragedy. Despite staggering evidence to the contrary in our own church, any system which promotes elitism, which says that one group or individual is better than another, is in direct contradiction to the gospel message wherein Jesus proclaimed his image as that of a servant to the servants.

Elitism is oppression. It oppresses those it elevates and those it demeans. For the former it says you cannot fail; for the latter it says you cannot win. Further, elitism sidesteps accountability, taking refuge in its position of privilege by saying, essentially, do as I say, not as I do. It is a hollow luxury that Catholic women, in particular, and the People of God, in general, can no longer afford.

Accountability

Angie McDonough and Margaret O'Leary were upset. It wasn't that the slim young woman in the pants suit didn't approach the altar reverently. It wasn't as though she didn't genuflect before the Blessed Sacrament as she waited for Father to open the tabernacle and hand her a ciborium so she could help him distribute communion.

It was, as Angie complained to Margaret as they walked home from Mass that Sunday morning,". . . well, it was just the way she walked up there. . . you know, as if she owned the place."

Margaret nodded her head solemnly. "I know what you're saying," she said, patting Angie's arm reassuringly. "And what makes it worse is that she's a nun."

"As far back as I can remember, the church has been checking up on me," said Ruth Stowe, a Little League mother, to her neighbor during the second inning. "First it was 'Have you been a good girl?' which later translated into 'Are you a virgin?' Then it was 'Why aren't you married?' followed by 'Only two children?' (the implication being 'How?' and 'Why?'). I was constantly being held accountable for the state of my union, the temperature of my marriage, my involvement in the Mother's Club, and whether my boys tried out for the parish baseball team."

"And yet," recounts Irene Kincannon, a Montana mother of seven, "when I was detailing the activities of what was, for me, a typical weekend (providing a casserole for my son's swim-team party, attending a dinner given by one of my husband's clients, telephoning to line up food for a parish potluck), a visiting nun chided me gently by remarking that 'You mothers are so busy, I hope you find time to stay home and take care of your families and attend to *their* needs.'

"What she never realized was that everything I did that weekend was *for* my family. It's what's known as *living* where we come from."

Accountability.

In practical terms, what does it mean in the everyday lives of women in the church?

Until the last decade, nuns in the church had very little accountability to anyone in the outside world. They were answerable only to their religious communities, specifically their mother generals or mother superiors. In many instances, not even their own natural families could make even the most human demands on them (like requesting that they be present at the funeral of a father or mother, much less a member of the immediate family). When dire necessity required that a nun take care of an ailing parent, she had no choice but to leave the community where she was "released" from her vows.

Dependent as they were on their communities for permission of every kind, nuns became socialized into a parent-child relationship with their superiors, even down to such minutiae as having to ask for permission to take a bath or shampoo their hair.

This dependency took another form when they dealt with the world outside the convent walls. As consecrated virgins, nuns, swathed in their flowing habits, became objects of mystery and muted fascination. They were treated like fragile pieces of porcelain to be protected, deferred to, "taken care of." They evoked the noblest sentiments of chivalry and respect.

René, a former nun, recalls an event when, after a tutoring session in her home, a mother instructed her ten-year-old daughter to "walk Sister home" on a dark winter night so that Sister would be "accompanied." The mother's only concern was that the thirty-five-year-old nun be protected. It didn't occur to her that her young daughter might be frightened or, since they were city blocks, even in danger. Indeed, who was the child and who the adult?

Later, when nuns were given some freedom to venture into the outside world, the same expectations continued. Other people were still responsible for them. Everything from free health-care to vacation homes were donated to them. People never expected them to reach for a restaurant check or to pay full price without inquiring about discounts for religious. In the truest sense, their vow of poverty protected them from reality. They were the prototype of the helpless woman.

Since Vatican II, the changes have been dramatic. The distance covered by the nun who couldn't walk home alone and the sister who ascended the altar "as if she owned the place" can, in many ways, only be measured by light years.

For the majority of sisters who comprise membership in this country's approximately 600 communities, the change has come about in direct proportion to their decision to take control of their lives. It is a decision which reflects, in its fullest flowering, the vision called for in Vatican II.

In many ways, the contrast between the child-nun of twenty years ago and the assertive sister of today has caught most people, including the hierarchy, understandably off balance. Laywomen, struggling with their own search for identity in careers and life styles, are alternately confused and angry at both the risks undertaken and the strides achieved by women religious.

Also, as the consciousness of some laywomen in society is raised, they grow more and more impatient with women religious who, they feel, allow themselves to be scapegoats and thereby set back the status of all women by continuing to "buy in" to a system which supports their powerlessness.

Often this anger erupts in social situations where nuns are present and women in the room, recognizing them, begin to recall their early memories of sisters they had in grade school. Eventually they end up using the nun as a punching bag for all their collective grievances and negative associations with the institutional church. More often, however, sincere, devoted women like Angie McDonough and Margaret O'Leary, both of whom are single women and professional secretaries, feel caught in a crossfire. It is as though the child-nun of the past has suddenly become their authority figure, almost a priest-parent. Nuns, for so long predictable symbols of piety and consolation, have become yet another voice jarring their security in the one place they long for stability.

In effect, nuns in such organizations as the National Assembly of Women Religious and the National Coalition of Nuns, both of which have lay membership, have become the new challengers in the church.

On one level, the Angies and the Margarets of the church feel cheated. What right do the nuns have to contribute to the church's already rampant confusion? they ask. On another level, they are forced to deal with the fact that now that nuns, in terms of all outward appearances, *look* and, in many areas, act as they do, they will have to deal with them not only as equals but as competitors— educationally, socially, and professionally. How does their socialization as women in this society (a socialization that often fosters mistrust of other women) prepare them to deal with this? How can they receive these "liberated" women into their homes and lives with openness and ease? How can they, as laywomen, deal with a group who, in what seems like one giant step, has moved from a position of no accountability for themselves in the church to a call for equal accountability (whether they want it or not) for everyone?

"Sisters are not working for new roles in the church merely for themselves, but for women in general," says Sister Mary Luke Tobin, seventy, a feminist and former head of her community, her order, the Leadership Conference of Women Religious, and one of the few women observers at Vatican II. "That is why we wanted to get rid of our habits so that we could be considered women and not set aside as some special group.

"But there is a great desire on the part of many women, especially older laywomen, to keep us categorized and in a special group. They say, 'We don't mind your getting out of those hot and uncomfortable habits, but you must have some sign to show that you are a sister.' And I say, 'Why?'

"We categorize so easily. And we have to move away from this. It is important for sisters to be seen as individuals and as persons."

The question, as Sister Luke sees it, is one of freedom:

> One of the basic problems in getting women more fully
> involved in the Church's life is the resistance on the part of
> so many women to freedom. Many times people who are
> oppressed resist liberation because of their fears of freedom.
> Freedom is demanding.
> I agree with Betty Friedan when she says that women
> have been trained to passivity and docility. When you have
> been trained that way it is doubly hard to step forward and
> take on freedom with all its demands and responsibilities.
> Maybe this is another area where sisters, having had to
> do this kind of risking during our present experimental
> period, could be of service.[7]

Indeed, to what kind of freedom would today's nun call the
Ruth Stowes and Irene Kincannons? How would they suggest
that these women deal with the kind of accountability that has
been and is still being demanded of them? What valuable lessons have they learned that they can share with laywomen about
what it means to claim freedom for oneself as a woman and for
the status of women in the church as community?

The first lesson is that we are being called to a place where
we, as women, have never been before. It is a high-risk place, as
women religious can attest to. Casualties among their ranks led
to new questions and new answers, the results of which depleted
their numbers to a place where the median age for nuns today is
fifty-three years of age.

"In a sense, I feel like I stepped out of my skin when I took
off my habit," a Franciscan nun from Iowa noted. "But looking
back I see that the habit was really a protective suit of armor. On
the outside, it kept me safe from the world and the elements: the
sleet and the hail of the world's pain and suffering. It never really
touched me. Nothing touched me. I was safe inside."

"When I took off the habit after eighteen years, I felt naked, almost ashamed," said another sister from Kentucky. "I started having trouble with my breathing, but I know now that it was just that I was afraid. I stared at the stranger in the mirror with her awkward, newly-sprouted arms and legs, her fringes of hair dusted grey at the temples. I didn't know her. I wasn't even sure I liked her! Was making friends with oneself worth it? I wanted to go back to my old cell where I felt comfortable. But the lock had been taken off the door and I'd turned in my key."

They smile, remembering . . . the one, now white-haired; the other's face reflective, her flawless, unlined complexion a contradiction to her fifty years. "What would I tell laywomen about the experience?" they ask, shaking their heads, still amazed at their memories. "I would say that the first accountability to which we'll all be called by the Lord is to be ourselves. As a woman, I may look at another woman and think I know a good deal about her. But only she can tell me what she's thinking. I need her words to really know."

To speak of change, real change, churchwomen must first come to grips with the realization that they have spent their whole lives acting out other people's answers to what are really *their* questions. Consequently, women have even forgotten that they have voices. Perhaps that is why women cry so easily and often. Tears may be the only language through which they are able to communicate. "Going into crisis" by a woman in order to be heard and to get some attention may become a life-style and a way of relating, because it is the only time she is listened to with real concern.[8]

Perhaps freedom for churchwomen means learning to talk all over again. Indeed, the future of the church might very well depend on the ability of nuns and laywomen to sit down together as *sisters* and dialogue—a dialogue that might begin with an examination of the language we have been using to describe one another.

Midge Miles, a Massachusetts director of adult education, cautions against "using words that separate us. Our language can be dead wood: divorcée, broken home, unchurched, the religious, when it refers only to nuns. . . ."[9] She suggests that a term like "woman religious" can discourage other women from considering themselves as religious women. "It's hard for the laywomen that I work with to believe they can be 'religious,'" she says.[10]

Perhaps the greatest difficulty laywomen and nuns would encounter in dialogue would be finding courage for the process of confrontation. The centuries-old mystique of the nun's veil (whether in symbol or actuality) could well act as an impenetrable barrier unless both groups of women are willing to risk sharing both their positive and their negative histories as individual churchwomen. This includes sharing their disappointments, frustration, and anger with one another as women, as well as the mutual admiration and inspiration they have given and received over the years.

When asked what *needs* they felt they would like to express to one another in such a dialogue, women all over the country articulated the following areas of concern:

Leadership

If, indeed, women religious are the most highly educated group of women in the world, then by virtue of profession, training, and access, they are the logical leaders of women in the church. By virtue of their professed commitment as religious women, they are received and accepted in church circles where laywomen are not even invited. While in the past, their energies in dealing with the hierarchy were understandably centered on recognition, reorganization, and renewal in regard to their religious communities, now there is a new agenda which reflects the feminist consciousness and which demands attention. In light of that consciousness, for women religious to limit their qualities of leadership to the confines of community life is to deny their gifts to all people, as well as to reinforce the elitist concept of religious life which has drained so much of the church's creative energy for so long.

Laywomen stated over and over again that they are in desperate need of education and information regarding their options as churchwomen. Women religious, conversant with institutional channels, procedures, and processes, can provide them with practical understanding of such areas as hierarchical structures and canon law, which affect both their present status and future possibilities as women in the church.

In turn, laywomen can affirm and empower religious by calling for their presence in pulpits as preachers (where before nuns could only appear to ask for money for the missions). They can validate them as sensitive and authentic ministers by requesting that they co-preside at liturgies for families, especially in sacramental situations such as baptisms, weddings, funerals, anointings, and anniversaries. They can be called for and recognized by laywomen in crisis counseling at police stations and juvenile facilities; they can be requested as facilitators in family counseling.

Once laywomen are sensitized, they will respond to the enormous reservoir of talent and faith-presence of contemporary women religious (until now so often limited to educational environments for lack of being called forth by the community). Once this consciousness occurs, laywomen, aided by a cultural feminist consciousness which is already operative, will begin requesting the presence of women religious as ministers, an action which they will see as natural and just.

Only a woman can ask to be ministered to by a woman.

It is the only way change will occur in an institution which, historically, has regarded women as persons to be kept in their place.

Shared Information

In a society where upwards of fifty percent of the labor market is composed of women, there is much to be shared. But in a labor market which resonates with activity like the Equal Opportunity Employment Commission and Title IX, there is much churchwomen can learn.

Laywomen, dealing directly with these realities in terms of their economic and professional livelihood, have much to share with religious women in areas such as strategies, organization, and economic power. In addition to political considerations, laywomen can become invaluable data banks for nuns whose new ministries take them deeper and deeper into the marketplace.

Laywomen's professional expertise and experience in industry, business, education, science, and the arts can facilitate the work of many women religious who are attempting to work as agents of change in areas of social justice or in such fields as corporate responsibility, national security, and legislative reform.

The one consistent concern voiced by laywomen is in the form of a plea to women religious to *stop working for inadequate or unjust wages*! As long as a segment of the female population is willing to negotiate for donated services or to accept payment below the minimum wage, the level of economic progress for all women in the labor market is lowered.

In a system which celebrated denial, the vow of poverty can often be a smoke screen for women religious, preventing them from taking full responsibility for valuing themselves as persons. According to Maryknoll psychiatrist Dr. Maria Reickelmann,

MM, as long as this profound sense of self-alienation exists, good mental health is precluded and relationships are distorted on every level.

Family

A vital area of shared information which has only been discussed casually is that of insights from women who are currently raising families. Religious educators, both nuns and laywomen, have much to learn from these women: they are able to provide invaluable information from children as well as parents regarding society's pressures and demands on the family. All too often, mothers who are at home with families look at "the teacher" as the expert, never seeing themselves as resource persons ("teachers-at-home") with different but equally important channels of information to share.

Classroom teachers seldom see or hear what happens at the dinner table, in the car pools, at the slumber party; what emotional needs surface in family crises; in what concrete situations spiritual needs are expressed. Mothers at home should be encouraged to share these experiences and view this information as valuable, recognizing that, as the children's parents, their insights are not only important but critical.

Shared Professional Ministry

Still another area in the process of development is that of shared professional ministry, until now only an "official" possibility for the professed religious woman.

As laywomen discover and are affirmed in their gifts, they will be called by the community to exercise those gifts in a professional capacity. What effect will this have on religious women who must, in a sense, "move over" to let laywomen in?

Sister Kathleen Keating, in an address to the National Assembly of Women Religious, noted that:

> There are problems peculiar to the women's movement in the Roman Catholic Church. We are the only church with a large number (130,000) of women religious, many of whom are professional church workers and who for the most part have been paid on a stipendary basis. To some extent, sisters have at least one foot in the structure. On the other hand, more and more laywomen are seeking to become church ministers who must support themselves on a salary. Even in volunteer ministries, it is often the nun who is preferred since the tradition has validated her and not the laywoman. The ramifications of the problem are serious for they can separate women from women in the church.[11]

If we are to truly reflect the ministry of Jesus, then professional ministry for us should not be in terms of numbers but of needs. If we look at the fabric of contemporary society as reflected in the six o'clock news and the daily headlines, we will realize that in terms of healing and reconciliation, there is enough work for everyone. The harvest is indeed great and those who are "allowed" to labor are all too few.

The challenge is not to find work but to gain access and receive recognition for competence. The burden is not on those who are seeking employment but rather on those who refuse to hire. The scandal is that this occurs in the face of declining numbers of "ordained" ministers available to fill the vacancies. In the final analysis, it is the People of God who are punished, who become pawns in the clerical chess game.

For many, time is running out.

Sister Kristin Wenzel, OSU, pinpoints the long-range implications:

A major task that faces women in the Church is to create more equitable opportunities for laywomen and sisters alike to assume any ministerial positions in the Church *to which they are called and for which they are qualified.*

Unless the ministerial status of women in the Church is noticeably enhanced and appreciated, the future involvement not only of sisters but also of laywomen in the Church is in serious jeopardy.

Increasingly, their Gospel ministry will be exercised apart from the institutional Church.[12]

For, as Julia Sweeney reminds us, God continues to call us, whether we have a label or not.

CHAPTER SEVEN

Woman as Shadow

The Single Experience in the Church

"Whether she is single by choice or circumstance, the Christian laywoman increasingly refuses to have her singleness defined as a state of being which is incomplete, waiting, asexual, or dangerous. This is the heart of the confrontation that single women present to the contemporary church."

Grace Lamm
Young Adult Ministry
Resource Board
United States Catholic Conference

SINGLE . . . SEPARATED . . . deserted . . . widowed . . . divorced . . . women living in these situations cast shadows which represent their status in the church: they have presence but no substance. They walk in darkness because we deny them light. The total population of single women in this country (unmarried or formerly married) is over twenty-eight and one-half million.[1] The shadows these women cast on the church continue to grow. Institutionally, we grow discouraged trying to define them. Like shadows, they cannot be categorized into tidy theological cubbyholes. Consequently, we are embarrassed by them. They sense it and are overwhelmed by a nameless shame. Their failure? That they are somehow not connected to a man.

In our culture we as little girls learn that only the kiss of a prince will wake us to a happy-ever-after life; that a knight on a white horse will save us from a dragon; or practically speaking, that if we can just find the right man and marry him all our problems forever after will be laid to rest.[2] It is an attitude soundly based in scripture: "In our life in the Lord...woman is not independent of man, nor is man independent of woman" (1 Co 11:11). It is an attitude which has been legalized in a church where the only two models for women are those of virgin and mother. It is a reality in most parishes where the funding, the programs, the attention is on parents and children. Like the supermarket, everything in the parish comes in family size.

"Can't the church give people acceptance for what they are...and not merely in spite of what they aren't?" another wonders. "Doesn't the church realize that singles laugh and cry, triumph and fail, love and grieve, stray and seek answers and a sense of purpose and direction just like the rest of us?...

"Doesn't it care?"[3]

In a sense the church has neither the time, the money, nor the energy for singles. Its agenda centers on marriage and family; any deviations from this pattern cannot help but constitute a nuisance institutionally. For women, especially, the message is clear.

"Motherhood is the true Christian vocation of every woman," Elizabeth Schüssler Fiorenza reminds us, "regardless of whether or not she becomes a natural mother....Catholic women either have to fulfill their nature and Christian calling regarding motherhood and procreation, or they have to renounce their nature and sexuality in virginity. Consequently, this traditional theology has a place for women in the Christian community only as mother or virgin."[4]

For the woman who is divorced, the situation is even stickier. Although a divorce does not, and in fact never has, officially excommunicated her from the sacraments (except, in some cases, for those who had remarried without an annulment), she nevertheless continues to receive the message from some quarters that her marriage is indissoluble and that she is forbidden to date.[5]

Moreover, many women remain uninformed about even more recent developments. Sister Paula Ripple, FSPA, Executive Director of the North American Conference of Separated and Divorced Catholics in Boston, states:

> I consider it a tragedy and an unfortunate loss of opportunity for the entire Christian community that little or no instruction was done in most parishes following Pope Paul's November 1977 statement of the removal of the American law of excommunication for those who had remarried without a church annulment. Sensitivity to the separated and divorced on the part of the total community could have grown and deepened, had time been taken to review the original meaning of this law with its destructive interpretation over so many years, and with the implication of its removal.[6]

Of all, widows would seem to be unique among the singles population. They, at least, enjoy official respectability. But even a casual reading of the profile of widows in scripture should give all women pause.

> Honor the claims of widows who are real widows—that is, those who are alone and bereft. . . . The real widow, left destitute, is one who has set her hope on God and continues day and night in supplications and prayers. A widow who gives herself up to selfish indulgence, however, leads a life of living death. . . .
>
> To be on the church's roll of widows, a widow should not be less than sixty years of age. She must have been married only once. Her good character will be attested to by her good deeds. Has she brought up children? Has she been hospitable to strangers? Has she washed the feet of Christian visitors? Has she given help to those in distress? In a word, has she been eager to do every possible good work?

Refuse to enroll the younger widows, for when their passions estrange them from Christ, they will want to marry. This will bring them condemnation for breaking their first pledge. Besides, they learn to become ladies of leisure, who go about from house to house—becoming not only time-wasters but gossips and busybodies, as well, talking about things they ought not. That is why I should like to see the younger ones marry, have children, keep house, and in general give our enemies no occasion to speak ill of us. Already some have turned away to follow Satan. If a woman church member has relatives who are widows, she must assist them. She should not let them become a burden to the church, which ought to be free to give help to the widows who are really in need (1 Tm 5:3-16—New American Bible).

Today, there is a new category of the "younger widow." She is the single parent, a further refinement of the shadow woman. Currently, there are seven to eleven million single mothers in the United States with children under eighteen years of age. Ninety percent of the children in single-parent households live with mothers as a result of death and divorce. For the divorcée who is raising children, the average duration of child support from the ex-spouse is fourteen months.[7] One wonders what better qualifications for attention a woman-as-mother can have as a contemporary "widow-in-need"?

Added to these shadows are those cast by single women who, for a variety of reasons, have opted out of the virgin-mother model. They have chosen cohabitation with men. According to the U.S. Census Bureau, two million unmarried persons shared living quarters in 1977—double the 1970 figure.[8] In California alone, not only the most populous but the most pioneer, more people between the ages of twenty-one and thirty live together as singles than in marriage.[9]

It is no wonder that an eighty-year-old grandmother sighed deeply as she asked, "Whatever happened to the good old days when girls filled their 'hope chests' with linens and wore white gloves and prefaced all their questions with 'Mother, may I?'. . . ." This is a question with which both church and society struggle.

But for one theologian, Martin E. Marty, there is an even deeper question. "I may not, I do not, like those facts, but do I have the choice of turning my back on the people who are agents or victims of these changes?"[10] Churchman Nicholas Christoff's answer is "No." As an American Lutheran Church minister, Christoff has chosen to live in Chicago's largest apartment complex where he is pastor, counselor, and advocate for what he calls "the Church's major untapped resource—singles."

In his book *Saturday Night, Sunday Morning: Singles in the Church*, Christoff shares an experience which might have contributed to that decision. "While sitting in church one Sunday morning, I recall hearing the minister intone: 'We pray, Heavenly Father, that you will look down with *pity* upon the destitute, the homeless, the *single* and the widowed. . . .'

"How would you feel if you were one of the more than forty-eight million singles in America listening to a prayer like that?" he asks.[11]

To be a woman in the church means dealing with one set of problems, but to be a single woman is double jeopardy. Helene, an unmarried thirty-two-year-old systems analyst, describes an experience she had had while attending Mass in a large, seemingly sophisticated metropolitan parish. "The theme of the liturgy was Church as Family. . .a theme which is particularly close to me since I live far away from my own family and particularly miss them on Sunday mornings.

"As the priest continued to develop the theme of church and particularly parish as family, focusing on the importance of each member in terms of the unique gifts each possesses, I found myself filled with a warmth that brought me close to tears. It was as though all the longing and loneliness and emptiness that I so often feel in my singleness was being gathered up with a healing touch. I felt I had a purpose, a meaning, an importance in my human existence...a value that went far beyond my good education, my healthy paycheck, my attractive apartment, my circle of friends.

"All I could think of were the words of Jesus, 'Friend, come up higher!' I was part of a family. As a woman alone without a husband and children, I was qualified to be part of that family. All by myself, I was enough.

"I looked at the priest as he concluded his remarks and extended his arms towards the congregation.

" 'And now,' he said, 'to best express the real meaning of family, I ask all the married couples in the congregation to come forward and renew their wedding vows.' "

"Once again," she said softly, "the door had been slammed shut."

What is it like to be a single woman in church society? Is the "freedom" of the single woman a myth or a reality?

Beth, an attractive teacher in her early thirties, speaks of a prevailing attitude that is a subtle, but unrelenting, pressure which, she says, "like water on the rock, wears you down.

"The assumption is that, *of course*, a woman wants to be married, and if she is not, it is because there is something basically the matter with her; she is either neurotic, frigid, weird, 'bitchy,' unlovable, an all-round loser, or all of the above."

Laura, a twenty-five-year-old sales-marketing coordinator, sums up this attitude by saying, "Catholic girls grow up to be wives and mothers. Period. End of sentence. This assumption is acted upon by well-meaning friends who, certain that you feel 'deprived,' arrange blind dates for you. It is conveyed to you in the sighs of your parents who let you know, usually in front of other people, that they are reconciled to the fact that they will probably never have the grandchildren they longed for 'all these years.' "

The same implication comes in the mail in the stream of never-ending invitations to bridal teas, wedding receptions, and baby showers for classmates, chums, and long-lost cousins. And all the while, the media keeps reminding you how lucky you are to have so many "options." After all, to be single is to be *free*.

This "freedom," of course, depends on who is after you and for what reason: if it's a man, then you're supposed to be free to explore your sexual options endlessly and in infinite variety; if it's your employer, you're supposed to be free to work harder because your job is, after all, your "identity." This, of course, assumes your willingness and freedom to work overtime (unlike the "unfree" married woman who must rush home to cook dinner for her family).

If, of course, it is your paycheck as a single which gives you freedom, then you are resented for saving your money to buy a sports car, take a cruise, invest in a condominium or take disco lessons. And so, to "atone" for all this freedom, you must simultaneously, as a single, also be "available" to care for ill or aging parents; to provide bed and board for visiting friends or friends of relatives (as a favor); to donate time, money, and energy to worthwhile causes and charities (the church, of course, being paramount among them). All of which you are expected to do cheerfully, since you are not "burdened" with the responsibilities of a family.

The one thing you are not "free to be" is lonely, says Angela, a secretary in an advertising agency. "And there's no place you get that message more clearly than at church. Most parishes just don't know what to do with singles except shuffle them off to a once-a-month dance at the local lonely hearts club or ignore them altogether. There is the Mothers' Club, the Fathers' Club, the Altar Society (which meets in the daytime when most singles are working), or the chance to teach CCD on Saturday mornings (if you're not working). That leaves the choir if you can find a parish where liturgy is a priority."

Consequently, "adjusting to *not* being married is perhaps the most common problem of single Christian women. Most want to marry, and some feel inadequate, rejected, or even guilty because they have not. Our culture strongly encourages the woman to find her identity in relation to a man, and the Bible tells her that she has actually been created for him [Gn 2:18-24]."[12]

The fact is that many women, either through choice or lack of choice, will *not* marry. For an increasing number of those women, the choice is an active and continuing one. Many women are seeking challenges and enjoying success and creative fulfillment in careers, continuing education, travel, and new life-styles. Consequently, the option of marriage and family is not seen by all women as their only priority.

"To be a mother or to be single—these are decisions a woman makes," says Sister Mary Austin Doherty. "They're not the definition of her whole life."[13]

In *It's O.K. to Be Single*, Gary Collins notes that:

> We all know that most people do "walk in pairs" and those who are on their own run into frustrations because of their singleness. But married people have problems too. And the same God who created marriage never implied that the unmarried should be forced to resign themselves to a lustreless second-best kind of existence.[14]

Jesus said simply, "I have come in order that they may have life, life in all its fullness" (Jn 10:10). But he did not limit us in the ways in which we could give birth. Consequently, attitudes which define women solely in terms of their biological productivity do a disservice not only to the unmarried woman but to the woman who is or has been married as well.

"I am not saying that motherhood for the few years that children are at home is not a very important factor of any woman's life," says Betty Friedan.

It may be the most important factor! But motherhood occupies a woman for say, fifteen years. So if we continue to define women in terms of motherhood and if the education or the treatment of women in any theological institution or profession is still to be in terms of motherhood, we are saying to women "Go drop dead. You don't exist for most of your life."[15]

"Being single," says attorney-author Barbara B. Hirsch, "is not like having a cavity that has to be filled. Being single is simply a description of my personal status."[16]

The centering question for the Christian woman is not whether she is married or single, but whether she is responding to the Lord by using the gifts she has been given for the good of the community. Within that question there is the more immediate one: who is the Lord calling her to be *here and now, in this time and place*, not in her fantasy life, in her five-year plan, or in what she hopes will be this "pause" in her life until "Mr. Right" comes along.

Here and now! Is she accepting *responsibility* for the exercise of her gifts: for sharing them, nourishing them in prayer as well as in practice? Is she accepting the *challenge* of those gifts in terms of using them for the good of the community and the building-up of the People of God? Does she respect *herself* enough to respect her gifts, to see them as a reflection of her blessedness and *uniqueness*, the unmistakable sign of the respect which the Giver of those gifts has for her?

Does she truly believe those gifts were given unconditionally, without labels or price tags, in boxes that were *not* marked "For Singles Only" or "Open After Marriage"?

Does she truly believe in a God who loves us too much to put limitations on our creativity?

Linda Le Sourd reminds us that:

> the challenge to utilize their potential more fully for king-
> dom work is desperately needed for those [women] who
> regard themselves as unimportant and prefer to defer to men
> or more aggressive women. They need to be shown that by
> not fully using the gifts given them by God, they are actually
> robbing the Body of Christ of some of its strength and
> resources.[17]

Perhaps this is best understood by reflecting on the answers given to us by Jesus, answers revealed to us by him through his relationships with women. Where is it written that unless a woman marries and bears children, the Lord will not love her? When did Jesus make that a condition for friendship with the women who accompanied and supported him in his ministry? Do we have a single instance in scripture when Jesus asked a woman if she had done her duty as a woman and had been a good wife and mother before he agreed to listen to her, heal her, touch her?[18]

Didn't Jesus, in fact, deliberately reject and transcend all biological limitations in his response to the woman in the crowd when she called out, "Blessed is the womb that bore thee and the breasts that nursed thee"?

Swiftly, he replied, "Rather, blessed are they who hear the word of God and keep it." (Luke 11:27-28—Douay). Anatomy is *not* destiny, he said.

Over and over, Jesus talked about *friendship* as the model for relationship:

> You are my friends if you do as I command you. I do not call
> you servants any longer, because a servant does not know
> what his master is doing. Instead, I call you friends, because I

have told you everything I heard from my Father. . . . The greatest love a person can have for his friends is to give his life for them (Jn 15:13-15). This, then, is what I command you: love one another (Jn 15:17). Love your neighbor as you love *yourself* (Mk 12:31).

When Rose saw the notice in the parish bulletin, she grinned from ear to ear. People sitting next to her in the church pew wondered what the silver-haired woman in the bright red coat was so happy about. Her smile was infectious. She had an idea.

Later that day she called the number listed in the parish bulletin; it was an announcement for a social club for senior citizens. The man who answered was friendly as he gave her information.

"You're a widow now, aren't you?" he wanted to know.

Rose was ready. "I'm a church widow," she said brightly. "I was a nun for twenty-six years."

"Sorry," said the man briskly. "We only take widows, and Lord knows, we've got enough of them! What we're really looking for is widowers. Too bad you're not a man!"

It's an empty feeling, loneliness. "We feel lonely because something promised has apparently been denied us. . . . We have the feeling that someone is missing."[19]

"Our society exhibits an extraordinary preoccupation with love," says Suzanne Gordon, author of *Lonely in America.*

Every other song of the radio laments love lost, praises love found, and makes it clear that you're nothing till someone loves you. It's not surprising, given this bombardment, that love (or its lack) occupies so central a place in our minds. For single adults, it's almost an obsession.[20]

The single woman is in a cultural pressure cooker. While the church compresses her in a double boiler labeled virgin and mother, it is the culture which turns up the heat. On the one hand, seldom a week goes by when someone doesn't ask or imply "how come a nice girl like you isn't married?" (It has been suggested that you respond by asking the married person why they *are*.) [21]

And while her credibility as a lovable human being is being questioned, she is also being exhorted by the women's movement to stand up for her rights by challenging her employer for a job promotion, filing for sexual harassment, or pressuring her bank to get credit, insurance, and loans.

Caught in the crossfire between traditional roles and contemporary pressures, she is often overwhelmed by a psychic loneliness that can be crippling. She does not know where her journey will take her; she only knows that she can never go back to where she was or who she used to be.

She turns to the church of her childhood, reaching out for some measure of understanding and healing, longing for the simple faith that once covered her like a warm comforter, listening for the echo of that faith's promises—"Come to me all you who labor and are burdened and I will give you rest" (Mark 11:28 —Douay).

And what is the official message from "Mother Church"?

If she is unmarried, she is told she must be a virgin.[22] If she is widowed, she is given comfort initially but is soon forgotten. If she is divorced, deserted, or separated, she finds she has been a victim, ironically, of both lack of information and of misinformation, both of which communicated to her that she was, in effect, an "outcast."

"For so long," says Sister Paula Ripple, FSPA, in her book *The Pain and the Possibility*, "good people have lived with destructive misunderstandings of an 1884 law. There was never a time when . . . divorce prevented a person's taking communion. The law applied only to the divorced/remarried."[23]

Yet each of these women is involved in a process of death and dying. The single woman, church-scripted for virginity until marriage, struggles against a culture which gives her more and more control over her body. To a church which claims to be both visionary and dynamic, she cries out for recognition and consideration of her options. She begs for breathing space, for relief from the guilt and shame she has been taught to feel because she is in touch with the needs of her body. She calls out for an explanation of the double standard which often paralyzes her: that she is at once both a gateway to the devil[24] and a "pearl of great price."[25] She suggests that the church's demand for her virginity is more often than not an indication of men's fear of her sexuality which, in turn, reflects their own lack of control.

For the formerly married—the woman who is single because of death, desertion, or divorce—the death is often literal, says Britton Wood. Death of a spouse is widowhood. Death of a marriage relationship is divorce. A dying marriage is the result of separation.[26] Each is also a kind of crucifixion. But Christ taught us that there is life after death.

The overwhelming message which streamed from Jesus on the cross was one of understanding and compassion. How would he have responded to the woman who found that her name had been dropped from the list of parish lectors right after it was announced that her husband had walked out on her and their three children "because he didn't want to be married anymore"? Would Jesus have grudgingly agreed to reinstate her with the proviso that if *she* entered into a "relationship" of any kind, he would of course once again have to drop her name?

What was his message to the Jews who put the letter of the law, the rigidity of legality, over the human concerns of the person who was outlawed, alienated, humiliated for situations beyond her control? What did he say to the ruler of the synagogue who chastised him for healing a woman on the Sabbath, a woman who had been so ill for eighteen years that she was bent over and could not straighten herself up? The ruler of the synagogue was incensed! *He did not see a woman, a person. He saw a rule.* And that rule had been broken.[27] The fact that the woman was innocent was apparently incidental!

Jesus' response was unequivocal: "You hypocrites! Any one of you would untie his ox or his donkey from the stall and take it out to give it water on the Sabbath. Now here is this descendant of Abraham whom Satan has kept in bonds for eighteen years; should she not be released on the Sabbath?" (Lk 13:15-17).

Jesus *could* have said to the woman, "Well, this infirmity you have is obviously due to poor judgment on your part. If you had taken better care of yourself, eaten the right foods, gotten the proper rest, exercised more, sought out medical help, you wouldn't have gotten yourself into this mess. *The condition you are in is your own fault!*

"However, out of the goodness of my heart, I'm going to heal you. But if you ever get sick again because you explored new ways to regain and sustain your health (new foods, medicines, climates), don't come around here and expect me to feel sorry for you!

"You're a loser! Unless you're a winner, we don't want you here!"

"You've got the question all wrong," says Anne, a fifty-five-year-old divorcée. "The question is not whether I left the church but whether the church left me."

CHAPTER EIGHT

The Priest and the
Single Woman in Ministry

"Until you eliminate the fear factor, you'll never have healthy relationships between women and priests. Not knowing women means basically distrusting them. The church has a male cult, a male mystique, where it is assumed that the men have all the knowledge and therefore all the power."[1]

Don Kohles

No DISCUSSION OF THE LONE- liness of the single woman in the church would be complete without a reference to the hazards single women in professional ministry encounter when they become involved in relationships with celibate priests. The majority of the women in these situa- tions are either present or former religious. An increasing number are laywomen trained in professional ministry. Many are single women who interact with priests in counseling or parish settings. Some simply meet socially.

"Relationships between women and priests involving inti- macy is something most people simply won't talk about," said Jean, a twenty-nine year-old artist and writer living in the Southwest.

"I believe we single women who work professionally or personally in church life are fooling ourselves if we don't admit that the celibate men who are our friends and colleagues are men whom we are capable of being attracted to and they to us.

"Ten years ago I wore blinders. I was a young woman in my late teens and early twenties who loved the church and the gospel and people. Priests were off limits; so were seminarians. It wasn't right to get involved. Ten years later I feel the same way— but the journey in between removed the blinders.

"There was something in my heritage that forbade me to admit to myself that I could be attracted to a celibate, that I could fall in love with a priest. The fact of the matter is it's no harder or easier than becoming attracted to any other man, married or single."

"It's as though people don't want to deal with the fact that priests and single churchwomen are human beings with normal needs and feelings," said an ex-nun. "Maybe the reason no one wants to hear about it is because it's not supposed to exist. It's time we as churchwomen shared our experience and dealt with it openly as part of our reality."

Part of that reality is the fact that a significant percentage of the tens of thousands of women who left the convent after Vatican II sought out continued employment in professional ministry. Many returned to work in church-affiliated offices, schools, and parishes. Although they returned to this setting as women unencumbered by vows and free to pursue social relationships, they did not expect to find these needs filled in their professional environments. They expected to find them in society after work and on weekends. What they found was a fast-paced, sexually-permissive, highly competitive culture.

"Most of the eligible men over thirty-five are divorced or separated," said Kathy, a former nun, whose experience is corroborated by her roommate Ellen, a thirty-two-year-old single laywoman. "As for the single men, they seem to want playmates but no commitment. It seems they all speak in the present tense; the future somehow doesn't exist for them."

In time, these women found themselves seeking out men who appeared to share their value systems and had a similar frame of reference. Because they worked with priests or encountered them with regularity, they found themselves turning to them naturally.

For single women who work in priest-staffed professional settings, there is the further disadvantage of not associating or working with single eligible men. Instead these women find that, unlike married men whose wives and families are able to provide emotional support for them, priests often have no legitimate avenues in which to experience and fill needs for intimacy. Consequently, priests welcome the opportunity to experience it by depending on the women with whom they work to provide them with psychological affirmation and support.

The trap is that the single woman is in the same situation. And if both she and the priest are simultaneously experiencing loneliness, the situation is doubly hazardous because both are vulnerable. It is, therefore, not surprising that both emotional entanglements and professional abuses often occur.

Further, since women have been socialized to be "rescuers," they often find themselves emotionally "hooked" into rescuing priests, professionally, with their brains and their talent. This often translates into the woman doing the priest's work for him. Some women welcome this opportunity. By attaching themselves to a priest and making themselves indispensable to him (as did a chancery office nun who assured a priest that she could be "very useful" to him), they exercise their need for power in the only way available to them: by manipulation.

"Consequently, there can be some deadly trade-offs," said an observer of one such situation. "The distortions which can occur in such relationships can be destructive in the extreme."

If the woman in question is struggling with loneliness, the temptation to a relationship which offers any alleviation of that loneliness can be overwhelming and easily rationalized. If the priest to whom she is relating has similar needs, the outcome is very often predictable.

Although relationships with priests and single women may differ, there is one point on which all of these women (nuns, unmarried, or formerly married) agree: "Falling in love with a priest is crazy," says Margaret, a thirty-five-year-old nurse/divorcée. "Everyone knows that a relationship with a priest is a dead-end street. It's asking for trouble. *I* knew it when I saw my relationship developing into something serious. But when I thought of what my life would be without him, I just didn't have the strength at that time to walk away."

One sixty-four-year-old grandmother who lived with her divorced daughter and three grandchildren commented on what she observed about her daughter's relationship with a parish priest who was a frequent visitor at the house because he was "close to the family."

"I don't know whether he was looking for a mother, a girlfriend, or a psychiatrist," she reflected. "All I know is that from the beginning, he expressed appreciation at being able to 'relax' with us.

"Because of his emotional needs (which included frustration with the pastor and the housekeeper), it seemed he used any excuse to drop by for a cup of coffee. My daughter is a loving, understanding person, and she responded. I'm sure she was flattered! Besides, he was 'safe.' He was a priest! How could she refuse him?

"In time, he stopped apologizing for 'being a bother' to her. It was obvious that she enjoyed and encouraged his being there. But I could see that his demands on her time and energy became greater and greater. The stress was on her, psychically and physically. But by that time it was too late. She was deeply involved with him emotionally."

An unmarried woman, a management executive in a large Catholic university, had a parallel experience of stress because of her relationship with a priest coworker. But because of her professional responsibilities she had to "walk on eggs" not to arouse suspicion.

"The guilt was overwhelming," she said, "and my work was beginning to be affected. I felt I was in danger of losing my equilibrium. I began to wonder if I stayed in the relationship because the guiltier I felt, the more I needed to punish myself. Finally, in desperation, I wrote to an organization called Mistresses Anonymous, founded on the same principle as Alcoholics Anonymous. I'll never forget how degraded I felt when I wrote that letter. What I was saying, in effect, was that I had lost control of my life."

Many nuns, both in and out of the convent, cite situations in the church and, in some cases, in their communities which they now feel might have contributed to their decisions to become emotionally involved with priests at the time. One nun describes her four-year relationship with a priest as a result of "not being honest with myself when it started.

"Looking back, I just let it happen. At the time, I was struggling with the seeming lack of caring and understanding in my own community. Everybody was 'into their own thing' and wanted their privacy. We even had our dinner on trays at night in front of the TV.

"When I met Jack and he was having the same experience in his community, there was a sense of comfort and security in our sharing. We spent more and more time together and our relationship just grew and grew."

"Maybe we were looking for excuses," said another. "Like priests, nuns very often found themselves off-balance. In the old days, we all had a clear-cut identity. Today, people aren't really sure how to treat a priest or sister, where to 'put them.' Do they treat religious as one of the gang or do they keep their distance? On the other hand, because their identity is blurred with others, priests and nuns sometimes wonder who they really are."

A former nun, who was a member of a religious community for twenty-two years, recalls the shift that occurred in the sixties, a shift which she says "is still going on in many ways.

"After Vatican II, everyone was 'liberated' and went into relationships under the guise of 'sharing religious experience' or 'encountering each other in depth in the Lord in liturgy.' The woods were full of women who got burned in those kinds of experiences," she said sadly. "In these situations, everyone forgives the priest, but no one forgives the sister. She doesn't even forgive herself."

Shadow women...

But perhaps of all single women in the church, none is surrounded by more folklore and conjecture than the parish housekeeper. She is either roundly praised or damned by one and all. She is both resented and revered by parish women because of her position of responsibility and control in the rectory. She is joked about, ignored, scorned and, in far too few cases, loved and understood.

"Hers is the loneliness of often being the only woman in a world of men...men who must keep women at arm's length in order to pursue their celibate vocations," said a former housekeeper. "If she is bereft of any other support systems, in time, this cannot help but affect her. Her own self-image can easily become distorted and she can come to regard women with suspicion and distrust."

Viewed in this light, it is easy to see how a housekeeper could internalize a negative image of women which men in this life-style often unknowingly communicate to her. On a deeper level, she might be unaware that often this can cause her to use her position to "punish" these men (by control or manipulation) for perpetuating the myth that she is inferior.

Yet her job description in the canon law books calls for a "superior woman."

The clergy shall take care not to have in their houses, nor to visit, women that may give reason for suspicion. They are allowed to have in their houses only such women concerning whom there can be no suspicion either on account of the natural bond, as mother, sister, aunt, or about whom on account of their character and more advanced age all suspicion is removed. It is left to the judgment of the bishop whether in any case a woman is to be removed from the priest's house, or the priest to be forbidden to visit a woman. If the priest has been admonished repeatedly and yet continues to be obstinate, he is presumed to be guilty of concubinage.[2]

"And yet, I wonder," says one former priest, "who will write the histories of those housekeepers who have gone down in history unheralded. . .those nameless women who gave everything and got nothing in return? No one speaks openly of those women who were more than 'housekeepers' to pastors. . .women who loved them and cherished them in fidelity, at great cost and personal suffering, for years and years.

"When people ask 'But who ministers to the minister?' they never mention these women. They never mention the fact that it was often the housekeeper who struggled to keep these priests on their feet when they were battling with alcohol or depression or even suicide. Many of them gave up the security of legal marriage and children to silently support these public men in their priestly ministry."

While there are as many reasons for relationships as there are individuals involved in them, there is common agreement that celibacy is a tightrope which must be negotiated, often precariously, by those who attempt to maintain religious vocations while simultaneously developing friendships which have the potential of jeopardizing that lifestyle.

The central considerations which must be dealt with in relationships between single women and celibate priests are those of accountability and responsibility. Addressing this issue in *Studies in the Spirituality of the Jesuits*, Madeline Birmingham, RC, asks in the case study of John and Mary, "By what right does the celibate offer her second place in his life in exchange for first place in hers? What happens when this apostolate takes him far afield? He kisses his friend good-by after taking up her time for several years and goes off. He is still celibate, still dedicated to the Lord, still committed to the Church and the Jesuits."

She stands at the airport holding a large empty sack in her hands. No husband, no children, no home, no future. Yet love is a pledge and a promise that speaks not just for today but also for tomorrow. Does the celibate understand this? Did she really understand what he could honestly promise in light of his prior commitment to God? Who does the giving and who does the taking?...

It troubles me that too few [spiritual] directors may not recognize that this is not John's problem alone. There is another real person involved....They seem to see them [persons] in two categories: those they serve and those who serve them....Some...speak as if the women (or woman) in their lives exist mainly for their benefit—to help them grow in affectivity. Where is their sense of personal responsibility and personal concern...?[3]

James J. Gill, SJ, addressing the same case study, provides an insight that women, especially, will find enlightening. Viewing relationships as a response to human needs, Gill centers his discussion on what need Mary is helping John fill. Aside from the need to achieve a "capacity for intimacy," a normal process leading to healthy personality develoment, Gill cities another need, one related to emotionally traumatic events:

This need sometimes becomes apparent just after one has engaged in intense and humiliating conflict with an authority figure; after the death of a beloved parent or close friend; or during a season of emotional depression resulting from the loss of one's position or failure to reach an intensely desired personal goal.

The relationship with the woman can fulfill a variety of requirements ranging from a mother substitute to a proof of one's virility.

To appreciate this reaching out to a woman in time of pain, it is useful to recall that down deep in every man there is a hidden conviction that his fears, loneliness, hurts, and every form of physical and emotional distress can in some almost magical way be allayed by a woman. How does this assumption arise? Through the personal experiences every one of us had as an infant and small child, when a woman converted our tears into laughter and our fears into confidence through the alchemy of maternal love. No wonder that in every man's unconscious there is generated a wish for the problem-solving, healing mother to return in the person of whatever good woman appears available when we find ourselves in distress and yearn for instant relief.[4]

It is doubtless this insight that led one observer to note that in the church there are only men and mothers.

Yet Gill's centering question—"What need does this relationship fill?"—should be the centering question for all single women involved in relationships with celibate priests. Is the relationship a matter of healthy friendship, an exchange which helps both people grow? Does it, for example, support and reinforce the concept of team ministry? Does it nourish spiritual compatibility? Does it provide breathing space for the other person to reach out to others in life-giving relationships? Does it respect the other person's privacy enough to know when to let go?

Or is it irresponsible in the sense that it fosters dependency? Does it initiate games in which the partners play "rescue me"? Is it challenging because the priest is "unavailable"? Does it reflect a woman's basic feeling of inadequacy and fear of permanent commitment to another person which may cause her life to be changed dramatically?

When a woman finds herself in a relationship with a man who has, in effect, stated publicly that he is unavailable, does she ask herself why she has made this choice and why she continues in it? Does she ask herself what "payoff" she receives by investing emotional energy in someone who, legally, has already rejected her? Does she interpret celibacy as nonexclusiveness and therefore noninvestment in relationships? If so, then she should also see herself as a target for exploitation; she is allowing herself to be used.

No matter how irresponsible the behavior of the priest-partner may be in this situation, it is the single woman who bears the burden for both the choice and its consequences. Socialized to be "at the service of others," many women unfortunately have often interpreted that teaching as the total relinquishment of their own needs.

One solution was suggested by a thirty-year-old unmarried woman. Reflecting on her relationship with a priest, she stated that "as women, we need to learn to be *aware* of our needs and take responsibility for our feelings.

"*That includes not being afraid of our loneliness,*" she added.

"The loneliness of the single woman in professional ministry or the loneliness of the single woman active and committed in church life is not inherently more or less than the loneliness of her married friends or single male-friends. No lifestyle saves any of us from common human loneliness.

"What lifestyle *does* influence is where we encounter loneliness, how we may choose to deal with it, and the obstacles and games we struggle with in between.

"One of the most worthwhile things I learned from this experience is that it's okay to know I'm needy, to be aware that I crave affection, to acknowledge that I find these men attractive on a variety of levels.

"But the critical thing is to keep myself honest about what I need! Only then can I take responsibility for my feelings. Once that happens I am free to make decisions. I, after all, *own myself!"*

"To walk knowingly into situations which are basically dishonest and therefore dehumanizing is to reflect self-hatred," said still another woman whose relationship with a priest left her "sadder but wiser. It is also to perpetuate the status of woman as servant in the church."

If single women are indeed shadows, then it is incumbent on all women to help dispel those shadows for their sisters. They might begin by asking for accountability from a church which sees singleness as "unfulfillment" for laypersons, while elevating it as "a special call from the Lord" for its religious.

If singleness is deviant behavior for dedicated laity, how can religious singles be exempt from that judgment? When celibates discount single persons, is it because they feel uncomfortable with people with whom they share that "deviance"? Is it because each time they confront Christian singles, they have to contrast their own labeled lives as single ministers (with institutional support systems) with those who struggle and survive on their own?

Maybe the time has come to recast a phrase that used to make our maiden aunts and spinster cousins shudder: the phrase "single blessedness." Why should singleness be seen as anything but blessed if it gives one the freedom to respond to a call to wholeness—to self-creation, self-discovery, self-respect?

Society prescribes for all unmarried women a single, unvarying goal—marriage. Once you take away that goal or reduce it to secondary importance, it is a rare woman who will not, at times, feel rudderless. She needs to discover by careful thought that she is free to pursue other goals, free to explore a world of potentially rewarding work and relationships. . . .

The more you dig out of your ruts, the more you transform loneliness so that it works for you, the more you put the effort of the search for the one-and-only into the search for your true self, the more you discover your goals and do work you enjoy, the freer you will become. And the final freedom of all is feeling free enough to be yourself—so that you can choose with conviction the life you want to live. . . .

As a single, the most important present you can give yourself is the exercise of your freedom. Far from being the second-class citizen society has always said you were, you are in a position to become truly a first-class person.[5]

As a Christian, this is the first destiny to which you have been called.

It has been said that although we do not have the church we want, we have the church that we deserve. Perhaps what has been absent has been the presence of single women—unmarried, separated, divorced, widowed, deserted—women who have walked in the shadows because, like the group huddled in fear in the upper room at Pentecost, they were without courage, without "tongues of fire" to light their way.

As a church, we must embrace these single women. As a family, they have been absent from our table for far too long. Together, we must call them from their shadows just as we are called by "the Creator of the heavenly lights, who does not change or cause darkness by turning" (Jas 1:17).

"You yourselves used to be in darkness," we are told, "but since you have become the Lord's people, you are in the light. So you must live like people who belong to the light" (Eph 5:8).

Religion

I'm a believer.
   I believe in kids
   Who ride their bikes
   Without holding on.

   I believe in the chances
   We take.
   To be complete
   For one moment
   With something we need.

   I believe in the crawling
   And struggling
   Of a baby
   Much more than I believe
   In his first step.

   I believe in trees,
   Especially willows,
   That do not try to fight the wind.

   And I believe in you,
   Whoever you are.
I believe.[1]

Merrit Malloy

CHAPTER NINE

Woman as Pawn
Examining Assumptions

"Without prophecy the people become demoralized."
(Prv 29:18—New American Bible)

WITHOUT EXPLANATION, Eleanor Anstey stands up on a chair in front of her students in a classroom at the University of Iowa. She smiles as she points out that, from that vantage point, things aren't always what they appear to be. From this height, on this "pedestal," she realizes very quickly that she is in a very confined, very restricted position. She has no freedom to move about in any way. She notes that if she does move in any way from this limited position, she is in danger of falling, of tumbling down and of hurting herself and the people around her. In a sense, she is partially paralyzed.

She wonders why anyone would choose to be in this place or to allow others to put her there. She wonders whether pedestals are really for the convenience of other people (rather than for the glorification of the person who has been placed on the pedestal). She wonders whether, under the guise of "honoring and protecting" her, others can, in this way, conveniently confine her, keep track of her, set her aside, or worse, get her out of the way altogether.

"Are pedestals the place for people?" she asks her students. She suggests that they stand up on the chair she is standing on and decide for themselves.

When a young feminist was challenged recently by a reporter to sum up the women's movement in a single word, she replied without a moment's hesitation. The word she chose to best reflect feminism was "Why?"

In increasing numbers, women throughout the country agree with that word and hear its echo in their own hearts as many of them stop, for the first time, to examine the network of assumptions on which their lives have been constructed. "*Why*," they ask, "does life have to be this way?. . . *Why* do people say those words. . .think those thoughts. . .expect those things?. . . *Why* do I?"

Churchwomen are no exception. They too, have their questions and categories. In the process of asking those questions and challenging those categories, they will come to see the cobweb of assumptions on which their lives have been constructed.

Assumption: If you respect a woman, you place her on a pedestal.

One of the assumptions that churchwomen are examining is that pedestals are for women. One of the conclusions women have come to as a result of that examination is that a pedestal is very often a camouflage for a cage. A cage imprisons. Within every prison is a victim or a criminal. Because of culture and circumstance, women have come to be seen as a combination of both. From Eve onward, women have been regarded as the source of all evil.

From the pen of an anonymous Irish poet of the sixth century, we read:

Eve

I am Eve, great Adam's wife
I that wrought my children's loss,
I that wronged Jesus of life,
Mine by right had been the cross.

I a kingly house forsook
Ill my choice and my disgrace
Ill the counsel that I took
Withering me and all my race.

I that brought winter in
And the windy glistening sky
I that brought sorrow and sin
Hell and pain and terror, I.

One of the ironies of history is that, as time passed, by internalizing the image of seductress, women became partners in their own victimization. As seductresses, women were seen to be the criminals. As battered women, abused women, raped women, they became the victims as well.

So it is today, that when, in asking for justice and equality in the church, their requests are seen as improper, even unlawful, they begin to feel like heretics or criminals. They become singled out as "displaced persons," "illegal aliens"; they are "persons without papers" (ordination), "without documents" (legality), victims once again.

Yet the church continues to proclaim that women are "revered," "cherished," "idealized," in a never-ending stream of words, pronouncements, and assurances which they support by placing her on a pedestal. Consequently, women are caught in a web of schizophrenia as they try to clarify, in terms of their own lives, who they are and need to be.

It is becoming critically apparent to churchwomen that no one, *especially the men in the church,* can give her an answer. Only she can discern, fathom, and clarify this answer for herself.

Assumption: Ordinary women aren't good enough to be models for one another—"you have to be a saint!"

Because she has been reared and educated in a patriarchal church which imposed its male answers on her (without ever asking her opinion, much less her approval), woman has no guidelines for her journey in self-determination in the church. And yet, she has only to look at her own life experience to find the road map to her own liberation. It surrounds her. *She has only to trust the significance of what she sees!*

Over and over again, when women were asked who their models were as they were growing up, they did not mention the Virgin Mary in her image of Our Lady of Sorrows or Mother of Perpetual Help, nor did they mention Joan of Arc burning alive at the stake. *They mentioned real life women in their own lives!*

The models for Sister Jo Louise Pecoraro, CSJ, who ministers in New Orleans' French Quarter, were two women in her own life: her Italian grandmother, whom she describes as "honest, direct, straightforward, yet accepting of people"; as well as her own mother, whose qualities of caring and neighborliness were exemplified in "a love of the church in all its fullness." The qualities of both these women are ones she tries to bring to her work with the street people, the elderly, and the handicapped to whom she ministers each day.

"My grandmother was my anchor," says Barbara Halloran, a forty-six-year-old divorcée and mother of seven children. "Without her example, I never would have had the strength to keep on going with the children. She always made me feel wanted and welcomed. She made me feel important. That was her legacy."

For Tosca Bulleri, who came to this country from Italy at the age of seven, the nuns who taught her in school provided a model of caring and love, which she remembers with gratitude to this day. "They gave me a self-confidence I desperately needed as an insecure child in a strange country," she recalls. "I came from a poor family and could not speak English. Yet their patience spoke volumes to me and provided the inspiration I longed for, the faith and the hope I needed as a child to survive."

Another woman who credits the strong support she received from nuns in school as a contributing factor in the professional success she has achieved in academia is Lee Hornberger, lecturer in mechanical engineering at the University of Santa Clara in California. "In school, the nuns always encouraged me and affirmed me; they always told me there was no reason on earth why I couldn't accomplish what I wanted to. They were successful women themselves and so naturally they were convincing models for me."

While these women, and countless others like them, prayed to, reverenced, and sought to emulate Mary, the Mother-Virgin, they drew their everyday strength from the flesh-and-blood women who cared for them, fed them, celebrated them when they were successful, wiped their tears when they were broken-hearted, and listened to their problems when they were lonely or afraid.

Scripture tells us: "Help carry one another's burdens: in that way you will fulfill the law of Christ" (Ga 6:2). *This is the essence of ministry, and it is what women have done for one another since time began.*

For one woman, there is an even more profound memory of being ministered to by a woman—a memory which has been passed down through generations of women. For Sara Gonzales

Segovia, it is the memory of first being blessed by her own mother, a centuries-old tradition in the Hispanic family.

"My mother always blessed the comings and goings of all the family members," Sara remembers, "even to the point of her own final journey when she was able to rouse herself one last time and bless us before she died."

Scripture tells us: "You are a chosen race, a royal priesthood" (1 Pet. 2:9—Douay). If churchwomen believe those words, they will strive not only for equal opportunity to labor (which the church has been only too ready to grant to them for centuries) but also equal access to all levels of ministry in the same church.

In her book *Womanpriest*, Episcopalian priest Alla Bozarth-Campbell writes of still another deep need on the part of women in ministry.

> Not only am I called to priestly ministry, but the lay person in me needs women priests. Priests need priests, too. I need the ministry of priestly persons who are women, to be an outward symbol to me of the part of divinity that is female, the part in whose image I am made.[2]

Assumption: Only men are able and qualified to be ordained ministers.

The only model of ordained ministry women have had is the male model, as witnessed by the fact that only men are allowed to receive the sacrament of holy orders. Nuns, although they have made a public profession of their vows, are nevertheless still denied that sacrament. In terms of their church status and "legality," they are laywomen.

Besides nuns, is there no other model of ministry for women? Is there no "simple Christian model" that can be provided *for* a woman *by* a woman? The kind of model women have been denied for centuries?

Ironically, simply on the basis of their physiology, the male leaders of the church are precluded from providing this model. Within the present structure, they cannot provide it, since oftentimes the areas in which women need ministering deal with problems relating to their own bodies and their own sexuality.

No man can fully comprehend what it is like for a woman to come to informed and prayerful decisions regarding the use or abuse of her body through the risks of artificial contraception, abortion, and childbearing while dealing, often simultaneously, with the ongoing physiological ramifications of menstruation and menopause.

Neither can men minister to women who have been victimized by rape, prostitution, abuse, or battering. There is no way a man can minister meaningfully to the female experience of mastectomy and hysterectomy. (Just as there is no way a woman can truly minister to a man who is sexually impotent.) Unlike a vasectomy, which is sometimes reversible, a woman's uterus or breasts, once removed, can never be replaced to give and nourish life again.

But, as we have seen, there is no need for men to *have* to minister to women in these areas. Women can and have ministered to each other in these ways since time began. *What is needed is for women to see this witness as ministry and to see that only they, as women, can provide these models and this form of ministry for one another.*

This does not mean that the male model of ministry, as we have known it, will become irrelevant or unnecessary. It will mean, rather, that the *model for ministry itself* will become enriched, expanded, all-inclusive. It will mean that a whole new model of ministry will arise which will include *the wholeness of the Body of Christ which is both male and female, one in Christ.*

It is not a question of men and women in ministry competing with one another but rather of completing one another. The unrealistic and inhuman pressure for the male priest to be "all things to all people" will be lifted from him. No longer will he find he must scramble to provide answers for questions (such as those dealing with the female life-experience) to which he cannot even relate! *The issue is not that women will turn away from men, but that they will begin to trust women.*

An analogy might be made in the field of medicine. Many women who have traditionally accepted, without question, whatever their male gynecologist or obstetrician told them about the condition and treatment of their bodies have now come to feel that they prefer to relate to a female physician in these areas. Not only will another woman be able to provide the necessary medical care indicated, but she will also be able to bring the added dimension of her understanding of the female life-experience to her professional relationship with her patient. Consequently, women who formerly felt uncomfortable with the suggestion of a female physician ("I just think I'd feel more secure if I knew a man were my doctor") have now come to see the value of a female physician who has an authentic understanding of her biological and psychological needs.

It is important to realize that this change of attitude could not have occurred unless a process of trust-building among women first had taken place.

This is not to say that these women will, in every instance, choose to relate only to female physicians in the future (and in the process, turn away from male physicians altogether). It simply means that they have opened themselves to a trusting experience with other women. In so doing, they have greatly enriched their current options for more wholistic medical care.

It is hoped that the journey of trust between women in medicine will be an object lesson of hope for women in the church.

Assumption: "The People" will never accept women as ministers. ("It's not our problem," says the church. "It's theirs!")

Because of a strong historical tradition and lifelong conditioning, there will be many women and men in the pews who will
still wonder whether women do, in fact, have the "qualifications"
for public ministry. It is fine, they will say, for women to "minister" to one another in common life-experiences, but are they
qualified and will they be accepted as ministers to the community at large?

A recent headline in the vocations issue of a diocesan news-
paper should provide the answer. It reads, "New Role in Church:
Associate Pastor Sister." The article pointed out that in the
diocese of Oakland, California, sisters now have responsibilities
that twenty years ago were only exercised by the ordained parish
priest. These responsibilities include coordinating liturgies; visiting parishioners in homes and hospitals; taking Holy Communion to the sick; providing spiritual counseling; preparing
parishioners for marriage, baptism, and other sacraments; helping with the administration of the parish; and performing almost
every ministry, other than celebrating the Mass and administer-
ing the sacraments.

One of these women is Notre Dame Sister Martin de Porres,
an associate pastor at Saint Bernard Church in East Oakland,
California. She stated that one aspect of pastoral ministry which
particularly appeals to her is liturgical preparation. "I'm a black
Catholic," she explained, "and the liturgy for me and my black
Catholic brothers and sisters is the heart of our experience."[3]

Outstanding examples of ministry are also provided by
laywomen in parishes. One such woman is Lois Joesten who
heads the Marian Visitors program at Sacred Heart Church in
San Jose, California. She coordinates a program of prayer and
eucharistic ministry to shut-ins, which touches the lives of close
to 100 people in that inner-city parish. Because of the efforts of
this former teacher and busy mother, the Marian Volunteers are
able to bring the Eucharist to those they visit and with whom
they often stay and pray.

Once again, women need only look around them as they sit in their churches on Sunday morning. As they do so, they should ask themselves not just who is the most visible minister (obviously the priest celebrating the Mass and consecrating the Eucharist!), but who is responsible for the everyday functioning of the parish. Who is responsible for the ministry of building community?

Through their gifts, women on parish teams and staffs are involved in crisis counseling and referral, teaching, and liturgical planning. Women, who comprise the majority membership in many parish organizations such as Mothers' Clubs, are building community. Their talents and skills and gifts are used in the parish to organize social activities which build community—the parish dinners, bazaars, bake sales, and rummage sales. These in turn bring in the money that helps build and support the schools, the hospitals, the activities in the communities. Many pastors admit, "I couldn't do without them." In many instances, women are truly the "heartbeat" of the parish in terms of prayer as well as activity.

To say that women do not have the qualifications for ministry is to demean both the people to whom they minister and the One in whose name they minister and to whose call they respond.

This is not to dispute the fact that the priest, by virtue of his "orders," has both the authority and training to perform certain functions and to be acknowledged publicly as the leader and "shepherd" of the community. But in point of fact, in celebrating Mass he is not engaging in a personal and private dialogue between himself and God. What he is doing, he is doing as a ministerial *representative of the community.*

The priest has his work, his gifts, his calling *as do all Christians.* Scripture tells us very clearly, however, that each of us has a similar calling, a unique but equally important responsibility— to share the gifts we have been given for the good of the community: "There are different gifts, but the same Spirit; there are different ministries but the same Lord; there are different works but the same God who accomplishes all of them in everyone" (1 Cor 12:4-6). More specifically, it continues,

> The body is one and has many members, but all are members, many though they are, of one body; and so it is with Christ. . . . All of us have been given to drink of the one Spirit. Now the body is not one member, it is many. If the foot should say, "Behold I am not a hand, I do not belong to the body," would it then no longer belong to the body? If the ear should say, "because I am not an eye I do not belong to the body." If the body were all eye, what would happen to our hearing? If it were all ear, what would happen to our smelling? As it is, God has set each member of the body in the place where he wanted it to be. If all the members were alike, where would the body be? (1 Cor 12:12-19— New American Bible)

Where, indeed, would the Body of Christ be without women? Women are "qualified" for ministry by virtue of the gifts they have been given, gifts which they are "called" to exercise for the good of the community. It is not really a question of whether women are *qualified* ("called") to ministry. (All are "called" at Baptism!) The question, rather, is whether or not they *accept the responsibility for exercising the gifts they have been given.*

No woman's ministry is "menial." Nor should it be considered "incidental." Nor is it, as one woman said of her year-long effort as fundraiser for a girls' school, "my little contribution." It is a vital contribution to the well-being and functioning of the church in this country today. It embraces and dignifies the woman who washes, starches, and irons the miles of altar linens as well as the woman who is president of a Catholic college in a large metropolis.

And when women say, "But I have no talents!" one reminds them that there is a ministry of listening. If anyone doubts the importance of such a ministry, one need only recall what it means to have someone who will listen to you when you are troubled, be patient with you when you are confused, encourage you when you are weak, and most important of all, be there to tell your good news to.

And there is always, at every moment, the ministry of prayer.

Perhaps one reason churchwomen tend to discount their contributions and be "embarrassed" by their gifts is that they have never received wholesome affirmation and recognition from their own peers, other women. Just as they have been socialized to seek their self-worth from men in society (fathers, brothers, bosses, husbands), so do they look to the men in the church to give them approval and a sense of well-being. In so doing, they have been denied a real source of strength, so far untapped and, therefore, undiscovered. They turn away from other women because from their earliest days they have been taught to see them as competitors, primarily for the attention and approval of men:

> In mixed-sex groups, most conversation is oriented toward the men. Women's comments are most often interrupted, overlooked or unheard because men are not used to paying attention to what women are saying. Women have colluded in this pattern, and they ignore other women too. One way to break this collusion is for women to support other women by paying special attention to what they are saying (regardless of whether or not it is agreeable to them) and reinforcing them so they will be heard and dealt with. This can be a very simple and powerful process once you begin to work with it. One example: after a woman begins to speak, another woman can watch the group carefully. If the speaker has been interrupted, the other woman can remark, "I think we

only heard half of your thought, what was the rest of it?" and help her to finish. Or if a woman who spoke was ignored, another woman can reinforce her statement with "Barbara really had an interesting comment on what we were discussing" or "I would like to hear what Edie had to say again; I'm not sure it was clearly understood." In any group, women must not permit other women's ideas to be dropped.[4]

Healthy relationships between members of the same sex, as well as the opposite sex, are something to be nurtured and treasured. But such relationships presuppose a deep-seated respect by both people, one for the other.

What is needed now is for churchwomen to develop that same respect for each other. They must seek out new ways in which they can relate to their sisters in the church as valuable, gifted persons, not as competitors for the attention of men (priests). They must affirm other women in the exercise of their gifts, whatever they may be. For some, gifts will be shared through training and education; for others, through actions grounded in faith and prayer. But all must be seen as gifted persons and encouraged and affirmed in their ministries.

This means also being open to women's ministries which are often beautiful surprises from the Spirit. An example of this is shown in the story of Verna Jarboe, a hairdresser, one of several laywomen featured in a filmstrip titled *Women's Gifts: Ministry as Self-Definition.*

Verna says, "When I look back on thirty-eight years of fixing hair and I think of all the women I've done and all their problems... With them, I've gone through pregnancies and marriages, living and dying, divorces and war... It's like I've been exposed to all their *soul.*"

Literally and figuratively, Verna embodies the symbol of the healing minister, through the gift of touch, the "laying on of hands." We see her in her first contact with her "ladies"— a shampoo to "wash all the worries out" (a kind of cleansing not unlike reconciliation). When she massages the back of their necks, she intuitively senses their need to be loved and comforted (anointed) because "they've been giving and giving and giving and no one has taken the time to give to them."

As she combs and brushes their hair, she shares their secrets, hears their "confessionals," admitting that "I have had women cry and some I cry along with. But they help me as much as I help them."

She is a composite of all the contemporary caretaker symbols to which people turn to solve their problems: the Crisis Hot-Line, the Dear Abby, the self-help manual. But she is real, she is there to *touch* them, even in silent prayers they never hear. "I don't have to get down on my knees," says Verna. "When my ladies come in I can say, 'Oh God, please, this one needs some easing up on. . . please make it easier for her.' When I see their hurt, I can say, 'Please, God, you know they've hurt enough. Just show them the way!' "[5]

Ministry is not just *giving*, says Rosemary Ellmer; ministry is also *receiving* the gifts of other people and *acknowledging* those gifts.[6] Further, says Dody Donnelly, to say "yes" to a person's tested gifts is to say "yes" to God.[7]

The words to the newly baptized in the baptismal ceremony are very clear: "You are priest and prophet. . . ." Christian feminists say simply, "If you won't ordain women, stop baptizing them!"

In the meantime, there is much that women in the church can do to prepare for that day. Examining assumptions is a way to begin.

CHAPTER TEN

Women in Church/Women in Society
How Do They Differ? What Can We Learn?

"Christianity cannot be considered in isolation from the general religious and cultural, psychological and sociological development of humanity."[1]

Paul Tillich

"Because of the close historical relationship between American women and church life, the future vitality of American religion cannot be considered apart from the contemporary women's movement."[2]

Reverend Barbara Zikmund

A WISE OBSERVER ONCE NOTED that the church has been carried on the menopausal backs of women for centuries. In this context, it is interesting to reflect on a report entitled "The Participation of Women in World Evangelization" issued by the Vatican Office for the Evangelization of Peoples. The report, issued by a commission overseeing missionary work, states: "In countries where women have made sufficient progress to warrant it, their role in direct evangelization and ministry properly so-called should be increased greatly." The reason given for this endorsement of an evangelizing role for women was that women's "potentialities. . . are being revealed more and more rapidly."

In this light, the report urges that women be given "full responsibility for decision-making" and be allowed to "play their full role in the parish team." Noting that women are already "permanently in charge of parishes with the authorization of the bishop," which includes officiating at marriages and baptisms, the report urged further study regarding women's official presence to the dying, including funerals.[3]

Historians, looking back on this period of church history, might reject the "rapid revelation" theory. Rather, they might consider the confluence of two events which led to the change of the centuries-old status of women in the church: (1) the shortage of priests caused by the absence of tens of thousands of men from the active priesthood in the last decade and (2) the women's movement, which is regarded by many sociologists as one of the most profound events of the twentieth century.

It is important that those of us living that history understand what these two phenomena reveal to us about our lives as Christians. How are they to be interpreted by a church which challenged itself during the Second Vatican Council "to recognize and understand the world in which we live, its expectations, its longings and its often dramatic characteristics"[4]?

How sensitive is the church to the needs of the women who stand at the crossroads of these questions—women of faith who struggle daily with their loyalty to a church which has not yet kept its promises to them in matters of justice and equality? How long will it take for the church to officially recognize the missionary work which is being performed by women in *this* country—women who, because of the official church's continued reluctance to include them in the decision-making process, feel along with others in the church that they are also on "foreign soil"?

What will it take for the church to realize how quickly one becomes enlightened when there is a basis for comparison in matters of justice, when one sees, for example, the treatment of women in secular society as compared to their treatment in the church? Since both claim a commitment to justice, the difference lies not in what churchmen say they support but what is, in fact, *mandated by law.*

As women try to rationalize the church's refusal to give them the fundamental power and/or right to vote, they compare this treatment with the rights they receive in the marketplace. There they are protected by such legislation as the Civil Rights Act of 1964 (Title VII), which prohibits employment discrimination on the basis of sex (as well as age, religion, race, or national origin).

They compare the channels they have for professional problem-solving in the church with those they receive in society from such groups as the Fair Employment Practices Commission and the Equal Opportunity Employment Commission.

They wonder why the church continues to refuse women—who comprise over half the church membership—the opportunity to receive an equal education in their seminaries, in sharp contrast with a guarantee assured, in society, by Title IX. (Title IX prohibits discrimination on the basis of sex in all federally-assisted education programs.)

Biblical scholar Raymond E. Brown, SS, makes some observations about untrained women currently working in parish ministry:

> If we are to ordain women priests, we must have full-scale seminary training for women. [Due to a shortage of priests] I have mentioned that already in some dioceses nuns are being invited to serve in parish ministry in an unordained capacity, but often these sisters are given only a quick pastoral preparatory course of six months or less. This is better than nothing in an emergency situation, but it means that they will remain second-class citizens when compared to male clergy who have had a four-year seminary course. Moreover, the pastoral inadequacies that result from a patchwork training of these sisters will be used as proofs that women make inferior parish assistants. No, women in the

priesthood means women in the seminaries. From my experience in a Protestant seminary that eagerly accepts women students, I would suspect that the presence of women would raise the intellectual tone of Catholic seminaries. . . .[5]

Women find this general educational ban on women as candidates for degrees in seminaries especially discriminatory in light of the church's own pronouncement against discrimination wherein:

> Every type of discrimination whether social or cultural, whether based on sex, race, color, social condition, language or religion is to be eradicated as contrary to God's intent. Such is the case of a woman who is denied the right and freedom to choose a husband, to embrace a state of life, or to acquire an education or cultural benefits equal to those recognized for men.[6]

Another cultural phenomenon which has enlightened churchwomen and served as a "survival model" is the movement for the passage of the Equal Rights Amendment. The wording of the amendment is brief and succinct: "Equality of rights under the law shall not be abridged or denied by the United States or by any state on account of sex."

Churchwomen note with interest that the official church refuses to take a stand on the Equal Rights Amendment (although the Canon Law Society of America officially endorsed the ERA at their October, 1979, meeting in Albuquerque, New Mexico)[7] despite the fact that the passage of the amendment would in no way allow the state to interfere with church policy regarding admission of women to the priesthood or certain ecclesiastical offices or performance of ceremonial rituals. This would violate the separation between church and state.[8]

Where it *would* affect the church is in its involvement in the many activities beyond its primary religious one: "support activities," such as schools, hospitals, and social service institutions, for which it receives large amounts of government subsidies and income- and property-tax exemptions. Canon lawyer Father Anthony Bevilaqua notes that:

> The Catholic Church, though organized for religious and not commercial purposes, would nevertheless be considered an "employer" engaged in an industry affecting commerce. On this basis also, it would be subject to legislation relating to social interests and policies.

The effect on the church by the passage of the Equal Rights Amendment, Bevilaqua states, "would be manifested mainly by the denial of government aid programs to such religious institutions, i.e., while the Equal Rights Amendment would not dictate a change in the programs or practices of any of these agencies, it may result in the denial of federal funding for them."[9]

Yet, while they note the church's stance of silence on the ERA, women are inspired with a new appreciation and awareness of the effort and staying power of those women whose energy and determination have been responsible for keeping the issue alive since 1923. It was first introduced in the Congress then and continued to be introduced annually for fifty years until 1978 when three states (votes) short of ratification, women were successful in getting Congress to vote for an extension of the ratification deadline to June 30, 1982.

Churchwomen acknowlege their debt to these women "survivors" and see them as models in their struggle. They celebrate their strength and tenacity. Yet, despite these examples, many contemporary Catholic women find it difficult if not impossible to maintain their personal integrity when they counsel their daughters to seek justice in their lives, careers, and relationships but not in the church. Many say that, "in all conscience" they cannot foster vocations in their children to such a church. The compromises such an action would involve are ones fewer and fewer women are willing to take. Nor, indeed, they have come to realize, should they. There are too many other options open to their daughters whom, they say, are being openly encouraged and welcomed in Protestant seminaries. (Forty percent of all theological students in seminaries are presently women.)[10]

"Women," says Sister Joan Chittister, "have come from being owned to being owners, from being kept to being keepers, from being led to being leaders."[11] And the most valuable lesson they have learned along the way is that *they are survivors and they are strong!*

Historically, it is as if they stand now on a stairway landing. They are resting before they ascend the next flight that looms before them and pausing as they look down at the flights which they have already climbed. They are only too aware now of the toll each of those steps has taken as they struggled upward on them. They have come to a new realization of how strong they are to be standing *here*, to have survived the climb at all.

On reflection, it seems to many that they have survived the impossible: They have survived the messages they have received about their bodies, the guilt which almost drowned their souls. They have survived the roles of servant, slave, institutional "sufferer." They have survived as long-suffering mother, silent sister, dutiful daughter, uncomplaining domestic worker. They have survived their silence, their humility, their subservience. They have even survived their own church history which, until now, has largely been a legacy of anonymity.

But the difference is that now, standing on that landing, *they see themselves as survivors!* They *know*, beyond a shadow of a doubt, that they are strong! And they know also that there is no turning back.

The seeds of survival were first planted, in this century, by Saint Joan's Alliance, an international organization of Roman

Catholic women founded in London in 1911. Considered to be the godmother of the women's movement in the church, Saint Joan's Alliance has gained recognition through its consultative status with the United Nations Economic and Social Council. In 1965, its members testified before the United States Senate on behalf of the Equal Rights Amendment. Its legacy to churchwomen throughout the world is inestimable.

But it was in the late sixties, when the documents of Vatican II received wide distribution, that new interest in women's status in the church increased in momentum. At the forefront of that movement were scholars like Mary Daly, (whose book *The Church and the Second Sex* is still considered by many to be the landmark publication of the period), Rosemary Reuther, and Elizabeth Schüssler Fiorenza of Notre Dame. Also in the vanguard were groups of nuns whose renewal, in the spirit of their founders, was mandated in the Vatican II Decree on the Appropriate Renewal of Religious Life (*Perfectae Caritatis*). Commenting on the experience, Sister Nadine Foley, OP, recalls:

> The directives of the Council emphasized that successful renewal and proper adaptation could not be achieved unless every member of the community cooperated. . . . Perhaps there is no greater testimony to the obedience of women religious than that they responded in full measure.
>
> The experience was painful, rupturing, having repercussions among all segments of the church. To become collegial . . . to scrutinize the signs of the times and interpret them in light of the Gospel and to adapt ourselves accordingly were processes frought with risk. But for those who endured, the effort was life-giving and freeing.[12]

In 1975, two events occurred which had an influence on the concerns of churchwomen: the declaration of International Women's Year by the United States which, in addressing the needs of women, focused an unblinking eye on the status of women in the church; and the convening of the first Women's Ordination Conference, "Women in Future Priesthood Now: A Call to Action," which took place in Detroit.

The following year, in 1976, also in Detroit, a conference was called by the United States Bishops on the anniversary of this country's bicentennial celebration. Entitled "Call to Action: Liberty and Justice for All," this conference provided an unprecedented opportunity for the People of God to articulate their needs and concerns in a public forum. The needs of women were mentioned in eighteen separate places and were relegated for consideration and implementation to the National Council of Catholic Bishops Ad Hoc Committee for Women in Society and the Church.

Because of these three events, justice issues for church-women surfaced, and their needs were given much visibility. Once again women's survival skills had been responsible for illuminating the issues, just as they are responsible for keeping the issues alive today.

My Name Is Waiting

I am a child born of the union of tradition and crisis. Sorrow is my grandmother; suffering and striving my aunts; begin anew my great-grandmother. I am a daughter not a son: My name is waiting.

My name has lived my life under the whip, under the lash; my name has lived my life within walls, within bondage; my name has lived my life through exodus, through sojourn.

I have waited in the desert of Syria, in the streets of Egypt, in the land of Babylon. I have waited in the cloisters of France, in the palace of the Oba of Benin, in the rice-paperhouses of Japan. I have waited in the Glens of Armagh, in the slave ships bound for hell, in the barrios of southern California.

I have waited in the tin shanties in Soweto, I have waited in the showers of Buchenwald; I have waited in the hills of the Dakotas.

I have waited in fields and vineyards, picking cotton and beans and grapes, cutting cane. I have brought down my hoe on hard ground; I have gripped the plow firmly; I have forced fruit from the earth.

I have waited in houses—washing, cooking, cleaning. I have sheltered the orphan, welcomed the stranger, embraced the lonely. I have lived alongside pain and disease, poverty and misery, anxiety and affliction. I have pleaded and hurt; I have known the coming of despair; I have given birth.

I have waited in the journey. My throat has grown parched thirsting for truth and justice. My feet have grown bloody cutting a path across the precipice, making a way where there is no way, coursing a road where there was no road. Righteousness was my guide. I have slept under gathering clouds with hope; I have rested near fresh water with faith; I have eaten and grown strong with love.

I have known blood and want and pain and joy. I have drunk water from the well; I have walked the threshing floor; I have been to the mountain top.

I am waiting.[1]

M. Shawn Copeland, OP

CHAPTER ELEVEN

The Bishop as Healer
Churchmen Challenge the Status Quo

*"What we have heard, what we have seen with our own eyes,
what we have looked upon and our hands have touched."*

1 John 1:1 (New American Bible)

WHAT DOES IT MEAN TO BE A Christian woman in today's world? To what is she called? For what purpose was she chosen? By whom is she challenged?

In a technological society where the only constant is change, the whole fabric of family life is experiencing new dimensions. Today, upwards of half the labor force is composed of women, and almost half of all children in this country have mothers who work in that market. Test-tube babies are a reality. The Equal Opportunity Employer is assured by law.

Because of phenomena such as these, Christian women everywhere are searching for authentic ways to witness in today's world and to make Jesus "the Believable One" to their families, their neighbors, and their coworkers—all persons who need the promise of God's love as never before.

This is as true for women in the church as it is for women in society where, increasingly, women suffer from what Adrienne Rich calls ". . . that female fatigue of suppressed anger and loss of contact with her own being."[1]

But old answers are quickly replaced by new questions. And the new answers to these current questions are evident in the mounting support and increasing witness being given by men and women throughout the country who are saying that equality for women in the church is not only an idea whose time has come, but a reality which is long overdue.

There are many ways to witness: by word, deed, demonstration; with one's time, money, energy, commitment; in faith and with trust.

But the heart of the matter is risk.

It is significant that more and more churchmen are coming forward to speak on behalf of justice for women, since it is they who, by risking, have the most to lose politically. It is a risk, however, which they have come to realize is worth taking because it concerns the question of human liberation for the entire People of God.

It is precisely this form of witness which speaks eloquently to many of the presence of the Spirit in the movement for women's equality in the church.

> Before women can fully respond to the role of protector of the human race and life itself, they must discover for themselves those qualities and life-styles which allow them to work in harmony with their true spiritual being and towards their full human potential. . . .
>
> Primarily, they must come to see themselves as the unique persons they are, and not merely the fulfillment of the expectations of others.[2]

These words, issued in 1974 by Bishop Leo T. Maher of San Diego in a Pastoral Letter entitled "Women In the New World," go on to speak of the price of the idealized woman:

> Woman has been idealized as the symbol of holiness, transcendent goodness, oneness, receptivity—and as extending this receptivity to the whole of her spiritual being.
>
> Beautiful as this may be, this image denies woman her sovereign dignity. In these representations, woman reflects a vision of someone totally for others (Pr 31:10-31). Her person

is not for herself but for mankind. What is defined is an exemplar, a divine idea in terms of symbolism, imagery, and poetry, which woman herself can only approximate.... The Church must always transmit as pure a Christian message as possible at the point of history at which it finds itself. It is not enough to review and reevaluate roles and models which have been proposed in the past. On the question of women's rights, it is not the ideal of womanhood that is at issue, but the person who is woman.[3]

Twentieth century woman cannot be expected to treasure those institutions that have limited her freedom, growth and opportunity in life.... Let us hear, then, those voices which vocalize woman's determination to assert her equality and profess her competence. Heedless institutions must inevitably pay the costs of indifference.[4]

The Pastoral Letter "Woman Intrepid and Loving" was issued in 1975 by Bishop Carrol Dozier of Memphis. He places churchwomen in an historical and cultural context:

Woman's coming of age was furthered by other human developments that have unfolded over the past few decades.... The civil rights protests revealed the personal and civil injustices that many deliberately and thoughtlessly imposed on others.... More and more women came to consider the civil right they had but could not enjoy....

In this age, the long and silent servitude begins to give way to the weight of justice where equality under the law can be asserted....

Like the universal movements for peace, for amnesty, for justice, the women's movement is international. Its influence can be a significant factor in the universal proclamation of the Word of God....

The evolution is irreversible; we are entering a period in which men and women are being called to become partners. . . . Neither men nor women will come to full personhood in a society where the gifts of one or the other are suppressed.[5]

I would just like to thank God for the women in my life, most of whom have been actively involved in the work of the Church.[6]

These words, written by Archbishop William D. Borders of Baltimore, reflect an openness which characterizes his Pastoral Letter "Women in the Church," issued in 1977. Part of that openness is evidenced in his willingness to assume coresponsibility with his fellow priests for injustices to women in the church. "I think we men have been taking women for granted and have been only on the receiving end of women's concerns too long. This is true in the Church as well as in society in general. . . ." Focusing on the needs in his diocese, Borders states:

I feel that the Archdiocese of Baltimore should offer leadership in recognizing the need for women in ministry and attempt to heal some of the pain caused by injustices to women in the past. . . .

First, I believe that all of us need to be sensitive and, as the case might be, to become more sensitive to the fact that some women have experienced inequities in the Church. In many subtle ways the men among us, clergy and lay, can suggest, perhaps most of the time unaware to themselves, that women are less capable of bearing witness and serving in the name of the Lord than are men. I would suggest that we clergy ask women what impression we give in our speaking about them or dealing with them.

I know that my own attitudes have changed in the past few years, and I believe that I have become more aware of this as I deal with women, both lay and Religious. I do not say that I am as sensitive as I should be.[7]

A serious form of injustice, not only in our society generally, but also in the church itself, is the underutilization of ethnic minority people and women in decision-making and other official roles.[8]

A specific plan of action to correct injustices toward churchwomen appeared in 1975, when Bishop Charles A. Buswell, then Ordinary for the Diocese of Pueblo, Colorado, issued a Pastoral Letter entitled "Ecclesial Affirmative Action: A Matter of Simple Justice." It announced a Diocesan Commission on the Status of Women, and called for the development of an affirmative action plan for "eliminating the injustice of discrimination (against women) in every parish and other diocesan unit in the church of Southern Colorado."[9]

The four-step procedure required parishes and diocesan units to (1) study the parish census to determine as nearly as possible the percentages of ethnic minority persons and women in the parish; (2) list positions in the parish which could be classed as policy-making or as bearing some official character, name the person holding those positions, and determine whether they are either women or minorities; (3) compare the percentage of women arrived at in Step 1 with that of Step 2; and (4) if the percentages do not match, draft a plan of affirmative action.

Speaking of the existing discrimination in today's church, Bishop Buswell's Pastoral Letter states:

This kind of discrimination was not present in the early Christian Community. It was surely absent in the attitude and in the ministry of Jesus. In spite of living and working in a highly structured class society, Jesus openly welcomed the participation of ethnic minorities (Gentiles), of the economically powerless (the poor), of the social outcasts (tax collectors), and of women.... Given the place of women in Jewish society at the time of Jesus, his attitude and conduct towards them is nothing less than revolutionary.[10]

Neither society nor Church can any longer tolerate the imposition of barriers in women's paths of growth.[11]

So wrote seven Minnesota Bishops in a Pastoral Letter entitled "Woman: Pastoral Reflections," a comprehensive, two-part document which was four years in the writing. It was released in March of 1979. Over and over again, the bishops call for justice for women in the church and society, presenting, in the process, a detailed list of situations in which discrimination occurs.

They note, first of all, that "We recognize that women's growth and dignity are often hampered by discrimination, sometimes deliberate exclusion, sometimes through inattention...." Calling for justice, they state: "Our pastoral concern goes out to all women in pain and alienation, to:

• the woman in poverty;

• the woman, alone in the home, fatigued from the constant care of young children;

• the woman alone because of widowhood, old age, imprisonment or confinement for health or mental impairment;

• the woman responsible for children without a father;

• the divorced or separated woman;

• the lesbian;

• the employed woman who does not receive just wages;

• the woman excluded from higher education, a profession or political office because she is a woman;

• the prostitute and other women who are victims of society's preoccupation with sex;

• the woman who is physically or mentally battered;

• the woman with an attitude of superiority towards men and children;

• the woman alienated from religion because she feels there is no place for her in the Church;

• the woman who hears God's call to serve through a variety of ministries or leadership positions but is blocked by tradition.

"We hear the cries of all women who are hurting, whose growth in love is stifled by society and the Church. We recognize that the correction of injustice implies ecclesial, political, and social changes; we commit ourselves to join in efforts to achieve justice. We pledge our care for women's growth, our attention to their concerns, our support in their search for justice, and our love. . . .

"For too long, society has treated women in a cavalier fashion. Guarded, protected and nurtured as though they were children, without consideration of their own abilities and desires, too often women have been guided into the roles of mother, daughter, wife, sister, teacher. Too often women have been valued for only those skills and strengths which support the work and strivings of men, or only tolerated in jobs for which there is no man willing or able . . . and then paid less than a man would be paid."[12]

Calling attention to the variety of roles and lifestyles which contemporary women occupy, the Pastoral Letter takes great care to affirm women in their struggle to raise families:

• "We recognize that legitimate family styles today also include two-parent families with both parents working outside the home as well as a number of single parent families.

• Our special care and concern go to the woman who carries the obligations of full-time employment outside the home along with the total nurturing responsibility for a household, when she alone earns the family income or must supplement it to avoid poverty. . . .

• We must publicly protest the injustice of the fact that the single parent who is a woman almost always receives lower wages than a man who does similar work. Not only is she handicapped by this, but so are her children. Therefore, we firmly support those laws providing legal recourse to women wage earners who are treated unjustly. . . .

• In two-parent families, partnership in parenthood and home management must become more common. And the partnership must be real, not theoretical. Well documented studies show that women still work disproportionately long hours in and out of the home because of the tradition that family and household are women's work. . . .

• We affirm the vital importance of the woman in every walk of life, as young, as old, and every age between. We affirm the vital importance of the role of the single woman, committed to service either as a professed religious woman or as a laywoman. . . .

• We caution all to re-examine our society's further tendency to define women primarily in terms of the family. This parallels the tendency to define men primarily in terms of their work. Since each person lives a complexity of roles, it is simplistic to focus on only one. . . .

• The Church should not only free its structure and attitudes for each woman, but should also welcome and support groups of women which strive for a solidarity of faith and love among themselves. Functioning within the Church, with support and encouragement, women should be able to find affirmation from each other, married women with single women, young with old, laywomen with professed religious women."[13]

While churchwomen rejoice at these words, there remains a deep reservoir of pain and hurt which many women feel deep within them—women whose minds and bodies have been scarred by the heavy burdens of exclusion, guilt, childbearing, and self-abnegation. And although they and their daughters are in the process of freeing themselves from these oppressive attitudes, the scar tissue from these wounds remains.

It was undoubtedly this reality which prompted theologian Dr. Elizabeth Schüssler Fiorenza to state that the *church must publicly confess that it has wronged women.*

Christian theology and the Christian community will only be able to speak in an authentic way to the quest for feminist spirituality and for the religious identity of women when the whole church, as well as its individual members, has renounced all forms of sexist ideology and praxis which are exhibited in our church structures, theologies and liturgies. . . . As the Christian community has officially rejected national and racial exploitation and publicly repented of its tradition of anti-Semitic theology, so it is still called to abandon all forms of sexism.[14]

While the Pastoral Letters quoted here speak to this issue, the Minnesota Bishops say the words: "If we, as leaders of our local churches, have ever closed ourselves to the Spirit's presence and power within women, *we apologize to them* and we seek the Spirit's forgiveness."[15] [Emphasis added.]

The five Pastoral Letters noted here represent eleven episcopal voices out of a combined total of 320 (including retired) bishops in the United States.

The gratitude with which these letters were received by the women and men working for justice for women in the church was matched by the fervent hope that the example of these eleven men would provide courage for their fellow bishops to follow suit.

The most convincing model of leadership is always one which involves personal witness: the transformation of words into action. An outstanding example of this kind of leadership was provided by Bishop Maurice Dingman of the diocese of Des Moines, Iowa. Addressing his priests in a Pastoral Bulletin, Bishop Dingman outlined a process which he had personally set in motion and in which he asked for the priests' participation.

Permit me to share with you what I have done and then ask for your cooperation in this effort to listen.

I met with a small group of women at my residence in Des Moines on February 8, 1976. It was a meeting in which we explained the issues in the Church relating to women.

The meeting brought a very fruitful exchange of ideas and agreement was reached to widen the dialogue and include all women in the Diocese. Consequently an invitation was issued by open letter to all women in the Diocese. A group of forty women met again at my residence on Sunday, March 28. Added direction was given to a continuing dialogue for the future. . . . It is the wish of the women who have met that the dialogue be widened to include, if possible, all the women of the Diocese. At this point in time these women already involved do not see themselves as spokeswomen for anyone. They think of themselves as facilitators to surface the interests and concerns of women.

What should be our attitude as Priests at this time? I would urge you to adopt my own attitude of mind and pastoral approach. That is basically one of listening. I don't [*sic*] think, indeed I am convinced, that this is not the time to set up any temporary or permanent structure or organization. *I would prefer to have widespread dialogue going on throughout the Diocese between the women and our Priests.*

I have hopefully set the example by personally inviting the women to my home. I have given them an opportunity to widen my horizons of the whole complex problem of Women in the Church.

You will be approached either as Pastors or as Regional Coordinators to participate in this dialogue. I envision the meetings around the Diocese occurring at the Regional level and at the parish level. There is also the possibility of inter-parish and inter-regional meetings.

When you are approached by groups of women I would ask that you respond with a willingness to meet with them. Give them every encouragement.

Out of this "constant and patient dialogue" (1971 Synod of Bishops in Rome) will come a deepening of trust and a sense of understanding. It is a process that is beginning and can produce very beneficial results. We are not in a position to predict the future but we can be certain that it will be productive of a "genuine Christian Community" (Vatican II).

I ask then that the Regional Coordinators be responsive to requests from women for dialogue. *I ask also that all Pastors be open to invitations to dialogue with women. I ask that you publicize these meetings in your parish Bulletins and give any assistance you may be in a position to give.* Encourage the women in your Region and in your parish to attend these meetings.

I would like to be present for as many of these meetings as possible. I want to listen to as many women as possible as we try to address their problems in our own diocese. I want the initiative to come from our Priests at the Regional and parish level. All I ask is that you do at your level what I have attempted to do at the diocesan level. I am more and more convinced that *we must take the initiative and invite this dialogue to take place. We cannot afford to permit a "credibility gap" to occur. We do so at our own peril.*

Permit, rather encourage, the women to organize these meetings to discuss their concerns. And then we must be present for the dialogue with them, *not in the style of informing or instructing them, but rather in the role of listening to them.* The time will come later for us to exercise our role of teaching. We are only beginning the process. *Now is the time to listen and permit their concerns to surface. We must under no circumstances dominate the conversation (dialogue) no matter how tempted we might be.*

May the "constant and patient dialogue" proceed in an atmosphere of prayer. We as Priests will be expected to add that prayerful and reflective dimension to the ongoing and developing dialogue. Our Holy Father refers to "the gentle action of the Spirit" in his recent Apostolic Exhortation of Evangelization.[16] (Emphasis added.)

In the meantime, the support for women in the church from churchmen continues to mount in a variety of places from both groups and individuals. An example of this support can be found in Priests for Equality, an international organization of 1,750 members, each of whom has endorsed a strong charter calling for equality for men and women in the church and society. Founded by William Callahan, SJ, this organization's membership represents a total of twenty-two countries.

In conjunction with the Quixote Center, also based in Mount Rainier, Maryland, Priests for Equality has initiated and sponsored publications dealing with women's ordination and issues relating to the feminist quest in the church. These include two studies: *Called to Break Bread? A Psychological Investigation of 100 Women Who Feel Called to Priesthood in the Catholic Church* by Doctor Fran Ferder, FSPA, and *Are Catholics Ready?: An Exploration of the Views of Emerging Catholics on Women in Ministry* by Maureen Feidler and Dolly Pomerlau. Because of studies such as these, the issue of women's ordination is raised from the level of speculation to that of well-organized and scientifically credible research.

Still more voices...

> I publicly acknowledge today my gratitude and appreciation of women and for their vocation in and gifts to the church. I believe the best way for me to express that appreciation is to continue to advocate their full and equal acceptance by the church at all levels.[17]

On October 2, 1977, in Richmond, Virginia, in an address on the subject of ministry, Auxiliary Bishop P. Francis Murphy of Baltimore expressed his hope for women of the future church:

> There is a future for women in the ministry in the church. It is promising. I make that pronouncement because I believe in the presence of the Spirit in the church and her members. I read the hope-filled signs of the times that launch us into the future. The consciousness-raising, through honest dialogue between women and men, women and women, men and men, through enlightened bishops and pastors... has to begin. I have a conviction that the future does not happen by chance but by choice. The future of women in ministry will be conditioned, and to a large extent, determined by the decisions we make today, by the plans we forge together.[18]

Bishop Murphy's public statement of support for women in future ministry could not have occurred without his own experience of consciousness-raising, an experience he shared earlier in his address:

> My attitudes toward women were deeply influenced by the closed and protective seminary formation I received. Along with my fellow seminarians, I was repeatedly told to avoid the company of women. At the time of ordination, I was again advised to avoid the intimacy of close relationships with women. . . . In subsequent years, I began to experience a gradual, mostly informal, but unswerving process of personal education. I began to analyze for the first time my attitudes, my tendency to stereotype women, my sexist language. Eventually I began to consider more seriously the place of women in the church. . . . My privileged assignment as secretary to Cardinal Shehan. . . gave me special opportunities to see at close hand the commitment of many women religious—often deeper than my own—to prayer, poverty, service to people, . . . [their] great skills of administration, special qualitites of love and community that were deficient in my own life. As time went by, I became increasingly impressed with the maturity and understanding about life that I saw in so many women—their openness to personal development, their hunger for spiritual growth. I observed these in married women and in single women, . . . in those who belonged to religious communities and those outside of them. I regard them as blessings. . . . [19]

Dominican Cletus Wessels, OP, an active proponent of human liberation in the church, cites clericalism as the major obstacle to the "developing reality of equality" for authentic ministries in the church. "Clericalism," he says, is "an attitude not of Christ and his apostles but of many priests and bishops in the church. . . the grain which must fall on the ground and die in order to bring forth the rich harvest of equality."[20] Though the yield is still measured by the handful, the harvest has begun.

CHAPTER TWELVE

Priests and Women

An Examination of Conscience
Through Attitudes

"When either men or women (black or white, rich or poor, young or old) condescend to one another, trifle with each other's importance, or question one another's value, personhood suffers. When men or women in the Church harbor these attitudes, the entire Church suffers." [1]

TO SPEAK ABOUT CHANGE IS TO speak about the unknown. But without change, there is no growth, and there can be no growth without risk. Perhaps the greatest risk facing the hierarchical church today is a prayerful examination of conscience in regard to its attitudes toward women.

The risk is great because it calls the decision-makers of the church to an accountability for those attitudes—attitudes consciously formed by training and education, as well as culture. These attitudes determine the behavior of priests in their day-to-day relationships with women. Unless these attitudes are held up to the light, they can never be truly examined as either positive or negative experiences which contribute to and affect, at the deepest level, the efficacy of one's ministry.

If we, as Christians, truly believe that we are being called to wholeness in Christ, then it is imperative that we test that call by trusting the Spirit to illumine the innermost recesses of our hearts and souls, our deepest fears and prejudices. It is critical that this examination begin at the grassroots level with the parish/family.

As the priest looks out at the faces of his people on Sunday morning, is he able to ask, in an attitude of surrender to the Spirit:

• How do I speak of women when I am in the rectory or in conversation with my fellow priests? What *words* do I use to describe them (useful, helper, nuisance, partner, workhorse, necessary evil)?

• Do I describe a woman most often as an object or a person?

• Do I relate to her as a co-worker, a threat, a Christian or a joke?

• What steps have I taken to examine my attitudes toward women which I learned during my seminary training?

• How have those attitudes affected me in terms of my personal and professional development as a minister of the gospel as well as a whole human being?

• Have I truly reflected on how many women it takes to support me in my ministry (secretary, school principal, Altar Society Board, Mothers' Club Board, housekeeper, organist, choir director, CCD director, CCD teachers, parish council members)?

• Am I willing to acknowledge to myself that without their support, I would be far less effective in my ministry?

• Do I call women by inappropriate names in order to ensure a paternalistic relationship with them? (Words like "Dear," "Honey," "Sweetheart" and phrases such as "You're a saint.")

• What "games" do I play with women in professional situations (secretaries, volunteers) in order to get work done? Do I use flattery or manipulation? Do I relate to them as mothers, co-workers, or rescuers?

• How often do I tell jokes that perpetuate women as sex objects?

• How often do I belittle women by calling attention to their natural bodily functions in a derogatory manner: "She's a nervous wreck! She must be having her period!". . . "She's impossible! She must be going through menopause!"

• Have I ever asked women to share their reflections on the church's teaching on birth control and abortion (matters which directly affect their lives as women)?

• Have I asked what effects these teachings also have on the lives of their daughters and sons, their entire families?

• As a visible leader in the church which professes justice and equality, how seriously have I taken the women's movement?

• Do I truly believe it affects the lives of the women who comprise over half the church's membership? Do I believe it affects the future of the church?

• If my Bishop wrote a Pastoral Letter on women calling for a correction of injustices, would I actively promote it in my parish? (See Bishop Charles Buswell: "Ecclesial Affirmative Action: A Matter of Simple Justice.")

• Would I consider such a letter a breakthrough or a burden in terms of the challenge it would present to me personally and professionally?

• How do I acknowledge my gratitude to the women in my parish who volunteer their time, talent, support, and energy: the CCD teachers, the Marian Visitors, the cooks and helpers at bazaars and church suppers, the members of the Altar Guild, the Mothers' Club?

• Do I mention them *by name* in the parish bulletins or from the pulpit? Do I remember them at Christmas or Thanksgiving, or do I honor them publicly at a special occasion (such as a luncheon or dinner) during the year?

• Am I irritated or responsive when I am requested to eliminate sexist language from the liturgy or replace sexist hymns whenever possible?

• Have I invited women to share their reflections from the pulpit on Mother's Day or on Marian feast days? Have I asked pregnant women to speak from the pulpit during Advent to share their reflections on what it means to be a bearer of new life or to speak for the rights of the unborn?

• What is my greatest fear (and therefore my greatest block) in dealing with women as persons? What steps can I take to eliminate those fears?

• Do I really believe that women are made in the image and likeness of God? How is this reflected in my relationships with them?

. . .

Someone once told me, "If you don't want to change, then don't pray."

Prayer teaches us to dream, to imagine the impossible. Prayer works against time, noise, language, pragmatism, inability.

It begins with an appraisal of what we are and where we find ourselves and then moves on to changing the situation and ourselves.

We pray and change is inevitable. If you don't want to change, then don't pray. . . .[2]

. . .

Women must examine their consciences as well. As they sit in the pews on Sunday facing the priest and the altar and surrounded by the People of God, women should ask themselves:

• Do I truly believe that women deserve the same opportunities for spiritual growth as men?

• Would I prefer to have a man or a woman give me spiritual direction? Why?

• If another person asked me for spiritual direction concerning a problem, would I feel qualified to help? What resources would I draw on to do so?

• Do I feel comfortable pointing out to a priest or pastor situations or instances in which I feel women are not equally represented or consulted? If not, why not?

• Do I feel just as comfortable about making positive suggestions of ways in which to correct these situations?

• Do I seek out and even initiate ways in which to bring about change for women in the church? What do I feel I have to gain or lose by such actions?

• Do I truly believe I am made in the image and likeness of God? In what ways do my actions as a woman in the church witness to this?

• When a pastor or priest asks me to perform a task or take on a project which I know will prove a severe inconvenience or hardship, do I refuse or do I accept (because "Father asked me" or "Since it's for the church, I'll manage to find the time somehow")?

• Do I actively support the pastoral work of other church women, calling attention to their accomplishments in public situations such as parish meetings, formal introductions, church bulletins, letters to the editor?

• When I speak about nuns and laywomen, what feelings do I experience, what words do I use? What impressions do I convey to a listener about my attitudes towards these women?

• Have I made any effort to dispel any past or current misunderstandings I have in my relationships with nuns or laywomen regarding lifestyles, values, vows or attitudes towards one's vocation as a religious, married, or single woman (widowed, divorced)?

• When I hear a nun is leaving or has just left religious life, do I offer her specific assistance during her readjustment period (e.g., aid with banking procedures, Social Security, car purchase and insurance, income-tax counseling, housing, health care)?

• When I hear that a woman is a former nun, do I ever express my gratitude to her for the years of service she gave in the convent—years in which she may have forfeited marriage and a family to teach my children, pray for my needs in the cloister, nurse me in the hospital?

• In my attitudes and relationships with the male clergy, do I expect too much of them (a priest must be pastor, accountant, psychologist, philosopher, management executive, sociologist, and "big Daddy")? Or do I expect too little (by feeling that every request is a nuisance and not worthy of attention: "Don't bother Father with this; he's so busy")?

• Why, indeed, do I expect too much or too little? How can I correct this situation?

• Am I comfortable with myself as a woman in the church today? If not, why not? By my actions, what am I doing to perpetuate or reinforce "woman's place" in the church?

• If I could change anything I wanted regarding women's roles in the church, what would it be? What do I need to do to make a change happen in my own life? In my life in the church?

· · ·

If you don't want to change, then don't pray. . . .
For prayer is the start of a motion, a continuing transformation and upheaval. Things are never the same as before and there is no going back.

Change means letting go, dying and rising. It is the continual paradox of death and resurrection which is experienced in prayer.

For prayer is a longing for change. It is asking that we become what God dreams us to be. If you don't want to change, then don't pray.[3]

Witness in the Rain

A little old nun sat
parked
in the falling rain
I said
"Your lights are on"
She looked
frightened
that someone disturbed her meditation
"Your lights are on"
She grimaced a two teeth smile
and nodded
"I understand"
I drove away
and still
her lights
shone into
the falling rain.

Gene O'Donnell

CHAPTER THIRTEEN

Women's Ordination
A Call to the Renewal of Priestly Ministry

"In God's plan every person is born to self-fulfillment, for every human life is called to some task by God....

"Endowed with intellect and free will, each person is responsible for his self-fulfillment even as that person is for salvation." [1]

Pope Paul VI

"Human beings have, in addition, the right to choose freely the state of life which they prefer. They therefore have the right to set up a family, with equal rights and duties for man and woman, and also the right to follow a vocation to the priesthood or the religious life." [2]

Pope John XXIII

IN NOVEMBER, 1975, 1,400 WOMEN and men gathered in Detroit to explore the issue of the ordination of women to the Catholic priesthood. At the close of that conference:

> ...more than 400 women stood up during a reverent and low-keyed blessing ceremony, indicating their call to ordained priesthood in the Catholic Church. They were married women, single women, women of religious communities. The atmosphere was one of prayer. Many participants at the Conference felt that the public acknowledgment of a deeply felt call to ordained ministry could not be taken lightly.[3]

The conference itself was a reflection of the seriousness with which women had accepted the invitation of the Second Vatican Council to share more fully in the responsibility of both building up the body of Christ and of developing their own God-given gifts more completely.

> In the years following the Council, women began listening more intently to the needs of the church and moved into positions of greater pastoral service. They increased their knowledge of the gospel message and earned advanced degrees in scripture and theology. They examined more closely the vision of equality expressed in contemporary church teaching and believed it. They listened with heightened awareness to the voice of the Spirit within them and heard a call.
>
> Perhaps it should not be surprising that the call which many women articulate is a call to priesthood.[4]

The groundwork for the Detroit Ordination Conference was laid at a meeting attended by thirty-one Catholic leaders the previous year. Those in attendance were concerned personally, or as representatives of supporting groups, with the issue of women in the Church.

The groundswell which originated from that first small meeting is still mounting. But the reaction from the official church, following the Detroit Ordination Conference, was clear. Clinical psychologist, Doctor Fran Ferder, FSPA, notes that:

> Some members of the Sacred Congregation for the Doctrine of the Faith were less than enthusiastic about the increasing talk of women priests. A year following the Detroit Conference, they issued the *Declaration on the Question of the Admission of Women to the Ministerial Priesthood*. This document reveals the discrepancy between the vision of the Second Vatican Council and the accepted practice of the

contemporary Church. Where the Council Documents stated that all women and men "enjoy the same divine call and destiny" and are "created in God's likeness, have the same nature and origin" (*Pastoral Constitution on the Church in the Modern World*, #16), the Declaration on the role of women indicated that women could not be ordained to the priesthood primarily because they do not bear a "natural resemblance" to Christ and it would therefore be difficult to see in the [woman] minister the image of Christ (*Declaration on the Question of the Admission of Women to the Ministerial Priesthood*, #5).[5]

Among the responses to that declaration by individuals, groups and organizations in the church was an open letter of dissent signed by twenty-three faculty members of the Jesuit School of Theology in Berkeley, California, one of six pontifical faculties in this country formally consulted by Rome on theological questions. The theologians criticized the Vatican declaration's conclusion as "not supported by the arguments or evidence adduced" and as "seemingly to try to stop a debate that should continue."[6]

In 1978, the Women's Ordination Conference convened a Second Ordination Conference in Baltimore. By that time its active membership had grown from 600 to nearly 2,000 and included women in Latin America and Canada. The difference between the first and second conferences was summed up by Sister Joan Sobala, SSJ: "In Detroit in 1975, we were orderly; we were listeners and went home with a vision. In Baltimore in 1978, we were in ferment; we participated and assumed ownership for the issue."

Taken to its logical extreme, the argument of "tradition" as the basis for the church's pattern of discrimination leads to absurdities, claim authors Nancy Hardesty and Letha Scanzoni. As examples, they ask the following:

• If women are unsuited to proclaim, preach, and teach the Word of God, then why are women permitted to teach women and children? Does this mean that we do not care if women and children are led astray? And at what age does a boy become a man?

• Why should it be acceptable for women to teach men in universities, even Christian colleges, and yet not in Church?

• Why do we hire women as directors of Christian education in parishes, giving them the responsibility for directing the formal religious education of future generations, which includes vocation guidance and direction?

• If women are supposed to keep silence in church (1 Cor 14:34), why do we let them sing solos, play musical instruments, and even lead choirs?

• Why are women allowed to write hymns, Bible studies, CCD curricula, magazine articles, and books which instruct men as well as women?

• Why can women serve family suppers in the church, but not the Lord's supper; . . . why can women bake the bread but not consecrate it during the Mass? . . .

• Most importantly, why was woman allowed the most intimate functions of bearing, nursing and nurturing the Son of God, and yet not be allowed, today, to consecrate his body and blood?[7]

While the debate on the ordination of women continues, there are some questions which need to be answered in light of the church's refusal to allow women to receive, along with men, the sacrament of holy orders. With the passage of time and the access of new information from behavioral scientists, we have come to realize that much of the church's theology which it claims stems from "tradition" is, in reality, rooted in fear.

Is there something sexual, for example, about the historic pattern of male pastor and the fact that the most active church people are female? If and when the priest is a woman, those sexual dynamics would be upset and recast.[8] Could this be the reason why the Catholic Church, which *chose* for twenty centuries to be intimately affiliated with a woman, still does not ordain them?[9]

Elizabeth Schüssler Fiorenza notes that in the light of cultural anthropology, it appears to be no accident that those churches which have a sacramental priesthood resist most strongly the ordination of women to the priesthood.

> The Christian sacraments are all rites which convey life... The sacraments, as rituals of birthing and nurturing, appear to imitate the female power of giving birth and of nurturing the growth of life. One would think therefore that women would be the ideal administrators of the sacraments.
>
> Yet there appears to exist a deep fear in men that women's powers would become so overwhelming if they were admitted to the priesthood and the sacramental ritual, that men would be relegated to insignificance. The demand of women to be admitted to the sacramental priesthood is, therefore, often not perceived as a genuine desire of women to live their Christian vocation and to serve the people of God but as an attempt to "overtake" the church. What men are often afraid of is that the change in role and position will not mean a mere shift in relationship between men and women but a complete destruction of any relationship or a fatal reversal of the patriarchal relationship.[10]

In the light of these questions, one can only marvel again at women's ability to keep the flame of their faith burning, to keep believing, to survive. Because of this, perhaps they have been involved in a far more healing ministry than the church has allowed itself to experience. Ada Maria Isasi-Diaz says simply, "I believe in a God of bread and roses."[11] Perhaps it is women's ability to maintain this delicate balance which has kept them spiritually alive for centuries.

Women have read all the rules and regulations and restrictions, the tomes of theology written by men over the centuries. Yet they know, instinctively, from their own experiences, that the most profound questions regarding the qualification for ministry (for both men and women) should be asked and must be decided in the human heart. One has only to look at the daily lives of ordinary men and women and ask, simply,

> To whom do you go when your heart is broken?
> Who takes the time to listen to you? And are they really willing to *hear* what you have to say?
> Do they experience you as someone unique and special and because of that know they have much to learn from you?
> Can you count on them not only to share your grief but also to rejoice with you when you are successful? Are they able to share your joy?

To care is to minister; to minister is to call. It is summed up in words of a woman who, upon hearing the prayers of Rosalie Muschal-Reinhardt,* called out to her spontaneously, "You are our priest, whether you admit it or not, because you call us to be alive!"[12]

---

*Rosalie Muschal-Reinhardt is a Coordinator of the Women's Ordination Conference. She holds a Master of Divinity from the Jesuit School of Theology in Chicago and is a wife and mother of four children.

CHAPTER FOURTEEN

To Whom Can Women Turn?

Groups Waiting to Welcome
Women in Today's Church

"A woman who views herself as the image of God is conscious of her great dignity, a dignity which bestows self-acceptance and self-esteem. . . . Wherever, within the church or society, a woman does not find liturgies, educational programs, social events or decision-making structures which meet her own and other's needs, she should work with persistence to establish them."[1]

The Roman Catholic Bishops
of Minnesota

ON DECEMBER 1, 1955 IN Montgomery, Alabama, the action of a single woman changed American history. When Martin Luther King asked Rosa Parks why, after a lifetime of law-enforced subservience, she decided to sit in the front of the bus, she said simply, "I was tired." Yet that one action, reflecting centuries of fatigue, provided the spark which set off the Civil Rights Movement in the United States and inexorably changed millions of lives.

In a sense, an increasing number of Catholic churchwomen sitting in the parish pews on Sunday morning are the Rosa Parkses of the contemporary church. They, too, have decided that they have the right to sit in the front of the bus. If they are denied that right, they will refuse to pay the fare. They will either choose to get off the bus at the next stop or, as in the case of the increasing number of Catholic women enrolled in Protestant seminaries, simply transfer to another line.

What the average woman in the pew does not know, however, is that her feelings of frustration and impatience with the church are shared by thousands of women all over the country—women who not only share those feelings but have decided *to do something about it by working together.*

There is not a lack of activity on behalf of women's rights in the church, only a communications gap. Throughout the United States, churchwomen are becoming agents of change by creating their own support groups, initiating dialogue such as is occurring between the Women's Ordination Conference and the National Council of Catholic Bishops Ad Hoc Committee on Women in Society and the Church, and moving into ministries in which their talents and spiritual gifts can be exercised.

Increasingly, churchwomen all over the country are taking their cue from society by learning to create their own support systems through "networking." They have learned that by sharing information, brainstorming, sponsoring professional seminars in human growth and development and by setting up their own consulting services, women are able to increase their options and thus more effectively change their lives. The success of their efforts can be seen throughout the country on a variety of levels.

"New England Journey: A Convocation for Women in Ministry" brought together 400 nuns and laywomen, "leaders and grassroots people," to discuss the topic "What Ministry Is in Our Lives and in the Life of the Church." It was sponsored by the Sisters' Senates and Councils of Women Religious in New England. The meeting was seen as a way for women to "bond together and support one another."

San Antonio, Texas was the scene of a workshop entitled "Doing Theology," which was sponsored by the National Assembly of Women Religious. Its purpose was to provide tools for grassroots church people whereby they could combine theological reflection with socio-economic analysis to address issues of social justice—in short, to ask the needed questions to free them from their assumptions of what is and what can be.

San Francisco's Committee on Women in the Church, sponsored by the San Francisco Priests' Senate, provides women with a support group in their efforts to develop their personal spirituality, to effect necessary reform in the faith community, and to provide women with ongoing studies in scripture and theology for personal and communal enrichment.

Chicago Catholic Women designs conferences such as "Do You Know Your Rights? A Ministry of Advocacy" in which they deal with the rights of and ministry to working women, pregnant teens, women in prison, gay women, abused women, Latino and black women, women in drug dependency, and women alone.

In northern Colorado, two laywomen are members of the Advisory Board of Religious Women, a group which acts in an advisory capacity to the Vicar of Religious regarding all facets of the nun's ministerial services in that section of the state.

A unique diocesan effort fostering women's ministries, the Order of Women, was established in Ontario, Canada, in the diocese of Sault Ste. Marie. Begun five years ago, it now has twelve mandated members. An extension of the deacon-training program involving the whole family, the three-year program (thirty weekends) now *provides single or married women* (whether or not husband is deacon) the *same training as lector, acolyte, and deacon.* The difference: where deacons are ordained and installed, Order of Women members receive diocesan mandates. Some women are involved in marriage tribunal work, others give instructions to catechumens, and some, with their ordained husbands, are codirectors of Catholic information centers. Home-study programs are involved.

The proliferation of these kinds of groups in the last several years is a sign of the times. They exist on every level from the local parish to the national arena.

Because they have undergone personal, spiritual, and professional renewal since Vatican II, women in religious life have a vested interest in both maintaining and increasing the strides all churchwomen have made in the last decade. This is reflected in the number of organizations sponsored by religious women whose stated goals include justice for women in the church. They invite laywomen (and men) to join with them in working for positive and creative change for the church community.

Membership in the following organizations is open to all women who share their goals and desire affiliation with a support group dedicated to working for justice issues for women in church and society.

International

Saint Joan's Alliance

Founded in 1911 in London, this international Roman Catholic lay organization has been in the forefront of the women's movement—first in the movement for women's suffrage and later in the issue of ordination for women to the priesthood. This organization has consultative status with the United Nations Economic and Social Council and has testified before the United States Senate on behalf of the Equal Rights Amendment.

National offices are at 435 West 119th Street, New York, New York 10027.

Women's Ordination Conference

An international organization of Roman Catholic persons, female and male, religious and laity, it focuses on the issue of the ordination of women within the context of a renewed priestly ministry. Projects include the establishment of local group networks throughout the United States (currently numbering 100) and the coalition among national groups which help to meet the needs of people. It invites ongoing dialogue with the bishops of the United States and the Vatican and publishes *New Women/New Church.*

National offices are located at 34 Monica Street, Rochester, New York 14619.

National

National Assembly of Women Religious

Formed in 1970, the Assembly is a grassroots movement and organization of women and men associates in the church. Its objectives are the promotion of a ministry of justice, particularly but not exclusively for women in the church and in economic systems, and *the reconciliation of differences between laywomen and sisters and between men and women.* The 1979 membership consisted of 2,000 individuals and seventy-three diocesan Sisters' councils. Concerned with oppression, which prevents people from making decisions about their own lives, NAWR has participated in such justice issues for women as the passage of the Equal Rights Amendment and the plight of battered women.

Offices are located at 1307 South Wabash Avenue, Chicago, Illinois 60605.

Las Hermanas

A national organization of nuns and laywomen of Hispanic origin formed in 1971, this group works toward being "actively present to the ever-changing needs" of Hispanic people through programs of cultural awareness and training for persons in ministry to the Spanish-speaking. Las Hermanas as a group supports each member in the appreciation and expression of Hispanic cultural and religious values.

National offices are at Post Office Box 4274, Denver, Colorado 80204.

National Coalition of American Nuns

Organized in 1969 by Sister Margaret Ellen Traxler, SSND, this coalition attempts to secure recognition and development for the role of women in the church and society, along with advocacy for social activism. Their newsletter provides membership with an updated listing of current justice issues related to women in church and society complete with names and addresses of groups and individuals such as legislators, government agencies, and corporations to contact to effect change.

National offices are located at 1307 South Wabash Avenue, Chicago, Illinois 60605.

National Council of Catholic Women

This federation of some 10,000 organizations of Catholic women in the United States was founded in 1920 to unite Catholic individuals and organizations. Its aims are to develop their leadership potential, to assist them to act upon current issues in the church and society, to provide a medium through which Catholic women may speak and act upon matters of common interest, and to relate to other national and international organizations in the solution of present-day problems. It is related to the National Council of Catholic Bishops through the Bishops' Committee on the Lay Apostolate and to the United States Catholic Conference of Bishops.

National offices are located at 1312 Massachusetts Avenue NW, Washington, D.C. 20005.

Network

This organization of women in Washington, D.C., is a Catholic social-justice lobby working for justice through national legislation. Focusing on issues which concern the poor and powerless, Network works to get Congress to legislate just laws which affect lives and change oppressive structures. A political ministry based on the theology of social justice, their services include lobbying, providing testimony at Congressional hearings, conducting phone alerts on significant legislation, and the sponsorship of publications, workshops, and legislative seminars.

National offices are located at 806 Rhode Island Avenue NE, Washington, D.C. 20018.

Regional

Chicago Catholic Women

An organization committed to prayer, education, and action, this group's purpose is to call the women of the Archdiocese of Chicago to full participation in the church. With a membership of 400 laywomen and nuns, CCW sponsors projects such as task forces on *Affirmative Action* for women employed in agencies of the archdiocese; *Outreach*, which identifies, authenticates, and expands ministries performed by women; workshops designed to sensitize grassroots groups concerned with women's needs in the church; *Pastoral Fund*, which aids in defraying educational expenses for women in various church-related programs or degrees; and retreats and prayer vigils for women in the area.

National offices are located at 1307 South Wabasha Avenue, Chicago, Illinois 60605.

The following is a list of resource centers and groups dealing with feminist issues within the church and society.

Institute of Women Today

A church- and synagogue-related women's coalition, the Institute was organized to search out the religious and historical roots of women's liberation. Catholic, Protestant, and Jewish women have designed a nationwide program to serve the universal sisterhood of women in new models of service and ministry.

For its regional and national workshops, the Institute calls on its faculty of 130 women lawyers, psychologists, historians, and theologians who are ready to help women interpret new models, new roles in law, theology, and values clarification through psychology. The sponsoring organizations are Church Women United, American Jewish Committee on Women, and National Coalition of American Nuns. Consultants include Abigail McCarthy, Doctor Margaret Carroll, and Dorothy Madden of the National Council of Catholic Women.

Since 1975, the Institute has been pioneering special programs for female prison inmates and currently has well-developed programs at four institutions nationwide.

Offices are at 1340 East 72nd Street, Chicago, Illinois 60619.

Quixote Center

A Catholic-based Justice Center composed of laity and religious, the center works in the areas of equality for women and men. It works closely with the Women's Ordination Conference and Catholics Act for ERA (incorporated separately). Projects include groups such as Priests for Equality. Issues deal with food for the hungry, the "Call to Action" process, the Karen Silkwood case, and spirituality for active Christians. Publications include two studies on the issue of women's ordination—*Called to Break Bread?* and *Are Catholics Ready?* The center provides workshops and lectures on these justice issues throughout the country.

Offices are located at 3311 Chauncey Place, #301, Mount Rainier, Maryland 20802.

National Sisters Communications Service

This national resource office was established to stimulate the effective use of mass communications in and by religious communities of women and men. It is a clearinghouse primarily, but not exclusively, for media professionals concerned with women's role in the church (religious issues, lifestyles, for example). The office provides consultations, workshops, publications, evaluation and communication-development programs, and some direct public relations services for religious congregations. It publishes *Media and Values*, a quarterly on modern communications and its impact on religious values.

The national offices are located at 1962 South Shenandoah, Los Angeles, California 90034.

Thanksgiving

I keep thinking about how and why and with what hands
People touch each other's lives:
The violence of bone and blood and muscle
It takes to make a reaching.
How much of a gift it is that any two persons
Straight lines toward doom intersect,
Become a charmed circle.
Amazing the patterns people make
By crossing each other's paths
Like black cats on this dark-night planet,
Amazing to say I LOVE YOU
HELLO.
O Lord I am not worthy that you should
That anyone should
Come under my roof
O Lord
But how glad.

Joanne McPortland

CHAPTER FIFTEEN

Women as Prophets
Pleas and Promises

"The church expects much from women for the accomplishment of her evangelizing mission. In the crisis we are going through, their role can be a decisive one, both for the humanization of civil society and for the deepening of faith within the family and within the eccelesial community. . . . . "[1]

Pope Paul VI

"To choose what is difficult all one's days
As if it were easy
That is faith."[2]

W. H. Auden

On OCTOBER 7, 1979, AT the Shrine of the Immaculate Conception in Washington, D. C., an event of profound historical importance and symbolism took place for American churchwomen and, indeed, for all the People of God. An American nun, Sister Theresa Kane, RSM, respectfully and personally challenged Pope John Paul II to "be open and respond to the voice of women in this country."

As president and the elected leader of the prestigious Leadership Conference of Women Religious, an organization composed of the heads of most women's religious communities in this country and *the only one officially established by the Vatican,* Sister Theresa's words carried both weight and strength.

"I urge you to be mindful of the intense suffering and pain which is part of the life of many women in the United States," she said at the beginning of the prayer service in the Shrine attended by 5,000 sisters.

Alluding to the Pope's repeated pleas for human rights which punctuated almost every talk he gave during his visit, she stated, "The church in its struggle to be faithful to its call for reverence and dignity for all persons must respond by providing the possibility of women as persons being included in all ministries of our church.

"I urge you, your holiness, to be open to and to respond to the voices coming from the women of this country who are desirous of serving in and through the church as fully participating members,"[3] she said.

Sounding the first negative note in a week-long pageant of parades, speeches, and celebrations which surrounded the visit of Pope John Paul II, her message stunned and surprised the national audience that heard her utter that challenge on network television. The risk Sister Theresa took in saying those words can only be matched by her courage in saying them. It is a measure of the recognition of "the suffering and pain of so many women in the United States" that she chose to do so—in fidelity to them and in truth to herself.

In the process, she stepped outside the realm of many Catholics' perception of "the good little sister," traditionally silent, obedient, and self-effacing. She risked alienating herself not only from the official church (whose ban on women priests had been articulated by the Pope a few days earlier) but also from a segment of her own membership, some of whom complained that she did not represent them and that her action was "inappropriate."

Yet a significant portion of the mail which flooded into the Washington offices of the Leadership Conference of Women

Religious supported her. And the Women's Ordination Conference in Rochester, New York, reported that they had received larger, more substantial donations in the days following Sister Theresa Kane's speech than they had received since their founding.

What is significant is that once again a woman, seeing a need, had the courage to speak up in an attempt to fill it. But John Paul II was not able at that time to respond as Jesus did at the wedding feast at Cana. Jesus filled that need out of his overwhelming love for his mother, although he protested that his time had not yet come. But women and men will continue to pray for the same kind of miracle, inspired in the same way as Jesus' action was—by John Paul's overwhelming love for the Mother of God.

What was abundantly clear on the occasion of Sister Theresa's words was that *the time has come for women.* And these women are not the stereotypical media caricatures of "women's libbers"—militant feminists who ostensibly advocate everything from bra-burning to unisex.

The woman who spoke those words represented the major superiors of approximately 600 religious communities of women in this country. The LCWR is an association whose purpose lies in promoting the spiritual and apostolic calling and works of sisterhoods in the United States.

We are speaking here of thousands of nuns who staff universities, schools, and hospitals; who work in parishes, dioceses, and chancery offices; nuns who minister to every segment of the population from rural America to the inner-city ghettos. Fifty of these women, wearing blue arm bands, stood in silent protest during the Pope's talk to them at the Shrine of the Immaculate Conception.[4]

But they issued a statement which explained why, for what and for whom they stood:

On the Occasion of Pope John Paul II's
Address to Women Religious

October 7, 1979

STAND UP FOR WOMEN

"Jesus turned to them and said, 'Daughters of Jerusalem, do not weep for me; Weep rather for yourselves and for your children.' " (Luke 22:28)

We Stand for Women:
- in solidarity with all women out of love and concern for the church
- to call the church to repentance for the injustice of sexism
- because we believe the church can change

We Stand Against Oppression:
- in a world where women and their children suffer most
- where sexism, racism, and classism are interrelated and morally wrong

We Stand to Challenge Our Church:
- whose sexist structures legitimize and reinforce sexist discrimination
- which repudiates the evils of anti-semitism and racism in the world, yet allows sexism and clericalism within itself
- whose moral teaching on sexuality ignores women's experiences
- which excludes women from major decision making
- whose sexist structures exclude women from sacramental ministry, thus limiting our potential for fullness of service
- whose refusal to address sexism within itself makes continued church membership a difficult question of conscience for many women

We Stand Because of a Moral Imperative:
- as nuns, and thereby privileged women in the church, we must raise the women's question
- as sisters in faith with Teresa, Catherine, Hildegard, and Joan who spoke their truth in loyal disagreement, we also call the church to conversion
- as Jesus ignored the societal roles of his time, breaking with religious law and tradition to bring the good news to the oppressed, the church must do the same today
- since Scripture and Vatican II mandate us to transform structures and policies of discrimination
- since sexist structures jeopardize the credibility of the social mission of the church

We Stand With Women:
- the sorrowing widow mourning her son (Luke 7)
- the woman bent over double for eighteen years (Luke 13)
- the woman seeking justice (Luke 18)
- the woman about to be stoned (John 8)
- the woman seeking healing for her child (Mark 7)
- the women standing beneath the cross (Matthew 27)
- the women proclaiming the resurrection (Matthew 28, Luke 24) [5]

On the occasion of the Pope's visit, there were fifty women who "took a stand" *for all women*, who stood for what they, as individuals, believed. But if their pleas continue to go unheeded at this time in history, their numbers will either grow or they will vanish. Having cried out with the collective pain of centuries, they will decide that the church, the Body of Christ, has no ears with which to hear them. And in despair, they will walk away.

CHAPTER SIXTEEN

Woman as Gift

"The future enters into us . . . in order to transform itself in us, long before it happens."[1]

Rainer Maria Rilke

No MATTER HOW MANY declarations are issued, position papers written, or laws mandated, equality for women in the church will take place only if and when women love themselves enough to make it happen. That is why the greatest challenge facing the female population in the church today is a public ministry to women: a ministry to women, by women, for women. It is critical because only women can declare, first to themselves and then to each other: This is who I am; this is what I need; these are my dreams.

Having examined their feminine models, studied their traditional and official "scripts," confronted the men in the church with their patriarchal sexism, compared their historical wounds, and celebrated their undisputed record for service and competency, they must now confront the greatest challenge of all: that of trusting their own questions.

But before this can happen, women, having acknowledged their rage and sadness, must now move beyond it. They must begin to realize that they can no longer afford to drain themselves of their awesome creative energy in grieving over a past which cannot be rewritten. Instead, they must transform and focus that energy on a dynamic and life-giving future to which the Spirit is calling them.

Only then can women truly challenge and discern their future as Christians by asking: As a woman, am I willing to accept the full responsibility for my God-given gifts by claiming the right to exercise them in all the ministries of the church? As a woman, am I willing to support, affirm, and encourage other women to do the same?

The answers to these two questions might very well involve not only the future of women but the future of the church itself.

What would a public ministry to women involve? First of all, the recognition that women must turn the time-worn pages of their church history and begin writing on a clean, new page. Because they will be bonding together *to seek justice in actions* as well as in words, they will be shattering the traditional molds set for them by the men who legislated their histories. Therefore, whatever is written on this new page will be written in their own handwriting, with their own words, in terms of their own understandings. They will be illuminating, for all people, the full range of human experience that is possible where the feminine perspective is included, a dimension without which the Wholeness (holiness) which we call God is incomplete.

For this to happen, women must truly believe that no change can take place for them until and unless they rightfully participate in the decision-making processes which affect their lives.

Dialogue

First, women must set aside time, space, and energy to look at where they have been, where they are, and where they, as Christian women, want to go. And they must do this in the company of other women who, like them, were never consulted on the life or death decisions which affected their minds and their bodies, their hearts and their souls. They must accept the challenge that is involved in the process of self-determination through self-definition; they must accept the fact that while *others may reflect on who they should be, only women can define who they are.*

The process of self-definition can take place only through dialogue: a dialogue which begins with women sitting down together in an atmosphere of prayer, mutual trust, and reverence for one another. They must share their feelings about themselves as churchwomen and, in light of these observations, how they would like their lives to change.

In the process, they must be willing to confront the ways in which they feel threatened or diminished not only by the men in the church but also by other women, be they laywomen or religious.

And because they are human, churchwomen need both the courage to speak the words and the humility to acknowledge their gratitude to those who have spoken them. M. Nadine Foley, OP, is one of these women:

> We women religious have enjoyed a privileged status in the church in the past. We have been respected, honored and cared for, even protected from the hard realities of the world which other people had to endure. It was possible for us to become the pampered children which, indeed, was the image many had of us. Our current struggle to assert our maturity and competence as adult women has been all the more difficult in the face of the "little nun," "good sister" stereotypes. . . . We now realize that our privilege is of a different kind. It is the privilege attached to the unique freedom we now have found and claimed as our own, not just for ourselves, but for other women as well, and indeed for all persons in the church. Many others, especially lay women,

are now demanding accountability from us. And they have a right to make such demands.[2]

Dody Donnelly, CSJ, is another:

We need to see non-vowed, single or married women not as possible sharers in our work, but to see ourselves as possible co-workers, supporters of theirs![3]

Discernment

Out of this process will emerge a consensus. It will include common needs and concerns as well as surprises. It cannot help but inform, encourage, and inspire women to a new awareness of their needs and problems as well as an appreciation of their strengths and sensitivities.

This process can take place among a small group in a suburban living room just as easily as in a parish hall or on the campus of a large university. What is important about the experience is that it sets a process in motion, a process which sensitizes women to the necessity and importance of owning their own needs and trusting their own questions enough to ask them aloud.

That is why it is critical that the dialogue take place *among* women. Only through such an experience can women begin to image themselves as ministers to one another. Only by sharing their fears, hurts, and questions do they give permission for other women to do likewise. Only by allowing themselves to be ministered to do they experience the healing power of other women and the knowledge that they are not alone.

Action

Once women are able to discover their needs by articulating them, they can begin to draw up a common agenda, a blueprint for action, appropriate to their condition and circumstance. This blueprint can then be presented to their local pastor or parish council, to a bishop of a diocese or the chairperson of a national organization. It must include a time line for completion.

What is critical for women to recognize is that no agenda is too small! Such an agenda might include a parish program for the equalization of male and female members on a parish council or in groups of lectors, or as extraordinary ministers of the Eucharist; a diocesan program involving the review and reevaluation of hiring practices and salary schedules for female employees; a request for continuing dialogue between bishops and women on a regional or national level dealing with women's concerns, which would include the needs of women in families.

It might be a request for a diocesan office of women's ministries, a clearinghouse for women's resources, or action to promote women's eligibility as candidates for degrees in local seminaries.

It might be a plan whereby women, be they secretaries or homemakers, are invited to be guest homilists, to share their reflections on the gospel in terms of their individual life-experiences. It could also include an invitation to women scholars to share their theological insights on issues facing the church and culture or comment on the contributions of outstanding women in Scripture or church history.

It could be support of an ongoing regional or national program of education and consultation (in conjunction with the Women's Ordination Conference) on the positive and negative attitudes which surround the issue of women's ordination in the church today.

It could be a support plan for the economic boycott already in process which prints and circulates "funny money": a facsimile dollar bill which is marked "Equal Justice Reserve Note—In God We Trust." On the reverse side, it reads: "To encourage the church to celebrate the gifts and calls of women equally with those of men in all ministries, I am withholding one dollar from this collection. I have contributed it to Women's Ordination Conference."

What matters is not whether the agenda women might design is modest or ambitious; what matters is whether it reflects the real needs of women and sets in process a motion whereby women are committed to be agents of change, because they believe in the promises of Jesus who ransomed them with his own blood.

The Sovereign Lord has filled me with his spirit.
He has chosen me and sent me to bring good news to
     the poor,
To heal the broken-hearted,
To announce release to captives
And freedom to those in prison (Is 61:1).

But for women to have named their needs and committed themselves to action is not enough.

Women are called to be dreamers as well.

We are at a truly holy time in history. As bearers of life, we are called to yet another level of love by the Lord: that of giving spiritual birth to future generations by being dream-speakers for those who have yet to come. The needs we reveal today and the plans we construct tomorrow are nothing compared to the "impossibilities" into which we will breathe life in the future. We have only to trust the life of the Lord within us to know that we will find a way.

That the flame of women's faith has continued to burn brightly through all the centuries in which she has been silenced is proof of women's ability to transcend the impossible. Women must come to appreciate that the greatest source of their confidence lies in their ability to survive, to keep on believing.

The unspeakable is what I want to say,

The unknowable is what I want to know,
The untouchable ones are the ones I want to touch,
The invisible ones are the ones I want to see clear.[4]

It is time, too, perhaps, to image a new kind of Eve, that is, a woman who sees her body as a reflection of divine creation and so is not ashamed of her nakedness; a woman who takes responsibility for her actions and neither blames others for her decisions nor allows the Adams of this world to blame her for their lack of self-control. She is a woman who sees self-knowledge as a blessing which frees her from her fears. She celebrates her "opened eyes" as a gift from the Lord to better help her praise his wonders in the world around her, to better seek out those who hunger for his love.

Sister Joan Chittister has said,

> I believe that we must realize that to be aware itself is to be sent. That is a sign of the sending! I am saying that consciousness is of the essence of prophecy [for] the realization of the message is really what commissioned every prophet. . . . They got the message whether they wanted to or not and were told to start.[5]

Women will not walk alone on this journey, for the Spirit has prepared the way.

"Faith seeking understanding" (*fides quaerens intellectum*) is the definition of theology given to us by Saint Anselm.[6] Through the process of self-definition, women will become more and more engaged in writing their own theology as they seek to understand the ways in which the feminine experience is nourished or diminished in relationship with the institutional church today. The formation of any theology requires a three-fold exploration: the lived experience of the people of God, the Christian tradition, and the contemporary milieu. It is in the dynamic interplay of these three dimensions within the light of the gospel that one can speak of an emerging theology.[7]

As in the writing of all theology, women will reflect on Scripture. They will set their thesis; they will clarify their terms and examine their assumptions; they will define the issues and ask the questions; they will gather the data and determine its importance; they will test it in relation to their experience of God. And finally, they will project its applications for the future. And from this, they will determine the who and what and where and when and how women will relate to tomorrow's church.

"And yet," asserts Rosemary Ellmer, who heads the Pastoral Care Department in a Catholic hospital, "although education allows you a calling card and credibility with people who are in power, education in no way can be substituted for personal religious experience. It is on the basis of one's own experience that one does theology."[8]

Women have never claimed that they have all the answers. But they also know that unless they are in touch with their *questions*, they will never find words and feelings to *express* those answers. They know, too, that only by expressing those answers can they choose to make them come true.

Again, this must happen in a sharing environment with other women. This is why it is critical that women provide themselves with the time and space to be dream-speakers, to fantasize about their participation in a church which embraces the feminine experience in all its life-bearing and life-giving possibilities. This sharing can provide the seedbed for new revelations and understandings. Because it is uncharted country, it can become holy ground.

Women should also begin to absorb consciously this process into their prayer life; they should begin seeing the fulfillment of their "impossible dreams" against the backdrop of the Lord's infinite palette of possibilities. "Because of your love for me and my faith in you, Lord, . . . hear my dream. . . ."

And whenever possible, women should reveal their dreams in the presence of other women. They should give them form and shape by describing their dreams in prayerful gatherings.

I have seen this take place in a room filled with women who have prayed together. It was awesome to observe the courage women summoned in the midst of that sharing: faith-filled women, who never imagined their dreams were of any importance, stood and, with sudden tears and trembling, whispered their deepest longings, filling the room with hidden treasures from their souls.

Yet the release of each dream gives birth to yet another possibility. By trusting our dreams, we trust ourselves; in trusting ourselves, we trust our feelings; in trusting our feelings, we trust the murmurings of the Spirit who resides in the wellspring we call our soul.

But perhaps the most important occurrence in our journey towards self-definition is the call to experience a new kind of vulnerability—to the Lord, to ourselves, and to those whom we seek to love. We are saying that on this journey into uncharted land, we cannot be certain of what we will find or whom we might encounter. We are embarking on a journey into a place in which there are no footpaths, no landmarks, no clearing. We are venturing into a land of mist. Faith is our only compass, but it will suffice.

> When women asked Jesus for a miracle, He never refused them and even pointed out the reason for his response: namely, women's faith. . . . So it was whenever women asked for help. Their faith prompted Jesus to grant their request. . . to bring this miracle to pass because women believe.[9]

Faith is vulnerabilty. Yet for women, without vulnerability, there is no possibility for forgiveness of and reconciliation with a church, which itself cries out for human liberation of its shepherds as well as its flock.

This much is certain: *To the extent that women free themselves, the church will be freed.* Once again it will reflect, with fidelity, the first freedom Jesus won for us, by his passion, almost 2,000 years ago.

But women, having survived their history, have learned an important lesson. Freedom is not a concession the church can ever grant them. As survivors, they know that, ultimately, freedom is a gift only they can give themselves.

. . .

Do not worry if the fight seems unduly great
and the work and suffering insupportable,
for the reward is great in proportion to them.

Look upon the beginning and end of all things,
our Lord Jesus Christ, who in joyful self-giving
endured the cross and was burdened with contempt.

Therefore, do not lose your confidence for an instant.
Run with love into the midst of the fight.
But run patiently,
for patience is most necessary
if you are to do the will of God with a pure intention.

God is all-powerful.
The things you have undertaken
are far beyond your strength to accomplish;
but he has promised to see you through
to victory by his grace.
And he is true to his word.[10]

Blessing of Lady Poverty

Notes

INTRODUCTION

1. Pope Paul IV, *Popularum Progressio*, March 26, 1967.

CHAPTER ONE: *Where Have Women Been?*

1. Donald Attwater, *A Dictionary of Saints* (Harmondsworth, England: Penguin Books, 1965), p. 65.
2. Ibid., p. 142.
3. Roger Gryson, *The Ministry of Women in the Early Church*, trans. Jean LaPorte and Mary Louise Hall (Collegeville, Minn.: Liturgical Press, 1976), p. 3.
4. Ibid., pp. 4, 5.
5. Ibid., p. 5.
6. Cecilia Preciado de Burceaga, Viola Gonzales, and Ruth A. Hepburn, "The Chicana as Feminist," in *Beyond Sex Roles*, ed. Alice Sargent (St. Paul: West Publishing, 1977), p. 270.
7. Joan Morris, *The Lady Was a Bishop: The Hidden History of Women with Clerical Ordination and the Jurisdiction of Bishops* (New York: Macmillan Co., 1973), p. 20.
8. Ibid., p. 24.
9. Ibid., p. 52.
10. Ibid., p. 45.
11. Ibid., p. 131. See also *New Catholic Encyclopedia* (New York: McGraw-Hill, 1967), 1:6-7.
12. Morris, *The Lady Was a Bishop*, p. 127.
13. Marcelle Bernstein, *The Nuns* (New York: Lippincott, 1976), p. 142.
14. Ibid.
15. Morris, *The Lady Was a Bishop*, p. 59.
16. Bernstein, *The Nuns*, p. 143.
17. Morris, *The Lady Was a Bishop*, p. 76.
18. Ibid., p. 82.
19. Bernstein, *The Nuns*, p. 84.
20. Ibid., p. 137.
21. Julian of Norwich, *Showings*, trans. Edmund Colledge and James Walsh (New York: Paulist Press, 1978), pp. 296-99.
22. "Beguines," *The Catholic Encyclopedia* (New York: Robert Appleton, 1907), 2:389-90.
23. Ernest W. McDonnell, *The Beguines and Beghards in Medieval Culture* (New York: Octagon Books, 1969), p. 479.

CHAPTER TWO: *Where Are Women Today?*

1. Bernice Sandler, as reported in *Stanford University Campus Report*, 10 March 1976.

POEM: *Requiem*

1. Thomas Roberdeau, "Requiem," *The Aurora Gifts: A Collection of Tales* (unpublished work).

CHAPTER THREE: *Where Should Women Begin?*

1. M. Timothy Prokes, *Women's Challenge: Ministry in the Flesh* (Denville, N.J.: Dimension Books, 1977), pp. 79, 5.
2. William E. Phipps, *Was Jesus Married?* (New York: Harper & Row, 1970), p. 176.
3. Leonard Swidler, *Biblical Affirmations of Women* (Philadelphia: Westminster Press, 1979), p. 343.
4. Nancy Friday, *My Mother, Myself* (New York: Delacorte Press, 1977), p. 130.
5. Ibid., p. 125.
6. Ibid., pp. 106-7.
7. Ibid., p. 100.
8. William E. Phipps, *Recovering Biblical Sensuousness* (Philadelphia: Westminster Press, 1975), p. 85.
9. Friday, *My Mother, Myself*, pp. 114, 113, 115.
10. Thomas Wolfe, *Look Homeward, Angel* (New York: Charles Scribner's Sons, 1957), Preface to Part One.
11. Prokes, *Women's Challenge*, pp. 44-45.
12. Pierre Teilhard de Chardin, *The Divine Milieu* (New York: Harper & Row, 1965), p. 66.
13. Joan Ohanneson, prod., *Women's Gifts: Ministry as Self-Definition*, filmstrip with Mary Ann Finch (Minneapolis: Winston Press, 1979).
14. Phipps, *Recovering Biblical Sensuousness*, p. 85.
15. Ohanneson, *Women's Gifts*.
16. Prokes, *Women's Challenge*, p. 80.
17. Ibid., p. 44.
18. Ohanneson, *Women's Gifts*.
19. William E. Phipps, *The Sexuality of Jesus* (New York: Harper & Row, 1973), p. 61.
20. Ohanneson, *Women's Gifts*.

CHAPTER FOUR: *What Do Women Fear?*

1. Marilyn French, *The Women's Room* (New York: Harcourt, Brace, Jovanovich, Jove Books, 1977), p. 70.
2. *Concilium Legionis Mariae/Legion of Mary Prayers* (Dublin: De Montfort House, 1969).

3. Marina Warner, *Alone of All Her Sex: The Myth and the Cult of the Virgin Mary* (New York: Alfred A. Knopf, 1976), p. 77.
4. Ibid., p. 14.
5. Ibid., p. 3.
6. Ibid., pp. 4, 7.
7. Ibid., p. 10.
8. Ibid., p. 19.
9. Ibid., pp. 18-19.
10. Ibid., pp. 105, 104.
11. Ibid., p. 153.
12. Mary Dorsey, "Mary Myths," *National Catholic Reporter*, 26 December 1975.
13. Warner, *Alone of All Her Sex*, p. 117.
14. Ibid., pp. 182-83.
15. Pope Paul VI, *Marialis Cultis: For the Right Ordering and Development of Devotion to the Blessed Virgin Mary* (The United States Catholic Conference, Washington, D.C., 1974), 2 February 1974, p. 27.
16. Anne Morrow Lindbergh, *Gift from the Sea* (New York: Pantheon Books, 1955), p. 56.
17. Patricia Noone, *Mary for Today* (Chicago: Thomas More Press, 1977), p. 141.
18. Elizabeth Schüssler Fiorenza, "Feminist Theology as a Critical Theology of Liberation," *Theological Studies* 36, no. 4 (December 1975): 625-26.
19. Doris Donnelly, "Sanctity without Sex," *National Catholic Reporter*, 24 May 1974.
20. Ibid.
21. Dylan Thomas, *Selected Letters of Dylan Thomas*, ed. Constantine Fitzgibbon (New York: New Directions Books, 1965), p. 29.

CHAPTER FIVE: *Women and Men*

1. Anthony Pietropinto and Jacqueline Simenauer, *Beyond the Male Myth: What Women Want to Know about Men's Sexuality* (New York: New American Library, Signet Books, 1977), p. 131.
2. Herb Goldberg, *The Hazards of Being Male: Surviving the Myth of Masculine Privilege* (New York: Nash Publishing, 1976), pp. 57, 64, 55, 69.
3. Marc Feigen Fasteau, *The Male Machine* (New York: McGraw-Hill, 1974), p. 18.
4. Goldberg, *The Hazards of Being Male*, p. 179.
5. Ibid., p. 183.
6. "Macho Men Die Much Sooner," *San Francisco Examiner & Chronicle*, 7 May 1978.
7. Goldberg, *The Hazards of Being Male*, p. 179.
8. Ibid., p. 188.
9. Ibid., p. 184.
10. *San Francisco Examiner & Chronicle*, loc. cit.
11. Goldberg, *The Hazards of Being Male*, p. 184.

12. Warren Farrell, *The Liberated Man* (New York: Random House, Bantam, 1974), p. 120.
13. Pietropinto and Simenauer, *Beyond the Male Myth*, p. 130.
14. Goldberg, *The Hazards of Being Male*, p. 34.

POEM: *For Every Woman*

1. Nancy R. Smith, *Images: Women in Transition*, compiled by Janice Grana (Nashville: Upper Room, 1976), p. 52.

CHAPTER SIX: *Who Are the Women in the Church?*

1. Lisa Marie Lazio, *Probe* (Chicago: National Assembly of Women Religious), October 1975, p. 4.
2. Patricia McCormack, "Quiet Revolution Thrusts Nuns into Mainstream," *San Jose Sunday Mercury-News*, 6 November 1977.
3. Daughters of St. Paul, *The Synodal Document on the Justice in the World—III* (Boston: Daughters of St. Paul, 1971), p. 14.
4. Nancy Hardesty and Letha Scanzoni, *All We're Meant to Be* (Waco, Texas: Word Books, 1975), p. 207.
5. Georgia Fuller, "Catholics for Women's Ordination: Confronting Roman Patriarchy," *Witness*, May 1978, p. 9.
6. Henri Nouwen, (Speech delivered at North American College, Rome, February 20, 1978), reported by John T. Muthig, *San Francisco Monitor*, 23 February 1978. See also Henri Nouwen, *Clowning in Rome: Reflections on Solitude, Celibacy, Prayer and Contemplation* (New York: Image Books, 1979), Chapter 2.
7. Luke Tobin, "Women Speak Out," *St. Anthony's Messenger*, March 1971, p. 28.
8. Carol Pierce and Janice Santacon, "Man/Woman Dynamics: Some Typical Communication Patterns," *Beyond Sex Roles*, ed. Alice Sargent (St. Paul: West Publishing, 1977), p. 103.
9. Margaret Dorgan, "New England Journey: Women Share Their Ministry Experiences," *The Church World* (Portland, Me.), 10 May 1979.
10. Helen Plasse, "New England Women Bond Together to Study 'Ministry in Our Church,' " *The Catholic Observer* (Springfield, Mass.), 4 May 1979.
11. Kathleen Keating, *Probe* (Chicago: National Assembly of Women Religious), September/October 1978.
12. Kristin Wenzel (Address to National Assembly of Women Religious, August 1978, Pittsburgh, Pa.).

CHAPTER SEVEN: *Woman As Shadow*

1. Nicholas B. Christoff, "Appendix B—Recent Census Report on Singles," *Saturday Night, Sunday Morning* (New York: Harper & Row, 1978), pp. 132-33.
2. Marie Edwards and Eleanor Hoover, *The Challenge of Being Single* (New York: New American Library, Signet Books, 1975), p. 30.

3. Christoff, *Saturday Night, Sunday Morning,* pp. 22, 5.
4. Elizabeth Schüssler Fiorenza, "Feminist Spirituality, Christian Identity, and Catholic Vision," in *Womanspirit Rising: A Feminist Reader in Religion,* eds. Carol P. Christ and Judith Plaskow (San Francisco: Harper & Row, 1979), p. 142.
5. Gerald D. Coleman, "Ministry to the Divorced and Separated," *Pastoral Life,* January 1979, pp. 38-39.
6. Paula Ripple, *The Pain and the Possibility* (Notre Dame: Ave Maria Press, 1978), p. 102.
7. Edwards and Hoover, *The Challenge of Being Single,* pp. 75, 73-74.
8. Curiosity Column in "California Today," *San Jose Sunday Mercury News,* 4 March 1979.
9. Martin E. Marty, "Foreword," *Saturday Night, Sunday Morning,* by Nicholas B. Christoff, pp. x-xi.
10. Ibid., p. xi.
11. Christoff, *Saturday Night, Sunday Morning,* p. 44.
12. Linda Le Sourd, "The Single Woman and the Church," in *It's OK to Be Single: A Guidebook for Singles and the Church,* ed. Gary R. Collins (Waco, Texas: Key-Word Books, 1979), p. 24.
13. Mary Austin Doherty, "Women Speak Out," *St. Anthony's Messenger,* March 1971, p. 7.
14. Gary R. Collins, ed., "Introduction," in *It's OK to Be Single: A Guidebook for Singles and the Church* (Waco, Texas: Key-Word Books, 1979), p. 7.
15. Betty Friedan, "Women Speak Out," *St. Anthony's Messenger,* March 1971, p. 30.
16. Christoff, *Saturday Night, Sunday Morning,* p. 98.
17. Le Sourd, "The Single Woman and the Church," p. 34.
18. Rachel Conrad Wahlberg, *Jesus and the Freed Woman* (New York: Paulist Press, 1978), pp. 19-20.
19. Suzanne Gordon, *Lonely in America* (New York: Simon & Schuster, 1976), pp. 25-26.
20. Ibid., p. 65.
21. Edwards and Hoover, *The Challenge of Being Single,* p. 35.
22. Sacred Congregation for the Doctrine of the Faith, *Declaration on Sexual Ethics,* issued 29 December 1975 (Washington D.C.: U.S. Catholic Conference, 1976), p. 7.
23. Ripple, *The Pain and the Possibility,* p. 103.
24. Leonard Swidler, citing Tertullian in *Biblical Affirmations of Women* (Philadelphia: Westminster Press, 1979), p. 346.
25. Matthew 3:45, 46.
26. Britton Wood, "The Formerly Married: The Church's New Frontier," in *It's OK to Be Single: A Guidebook for Singles and the Church,* ed. Gary R. Collins (Waco, Texas: Key-Word Books, 1979), p. 69.
27. Wahlberg, *Jesus and the Freed Woman,* p. 22.

CHAPTER EIGHT: *The Priest and the Single Woman in Ministry*

1. Don Kohles, "Ordination of Women: What Priests Think," *Oakland Catholic Voice* (Ca.), op. cit., 21 July 1975.
2. Stanislaus Woywod, *The New Canon Law* (New York: Joseph F. Wagner, 1940), p. 26.
3. Madeline Birmingham, "Concern for the Other," *Studies in the Spirituality of the Jesuits, Affectivity and Sexuality: Their Relationship to the Spiritual and Apostolic Life of Jesuits* (American Assistancy Seminar on Jesuit Spirituality) 10 (March-May 1978): 104, 103.
4. James J. Gill, "Responding to Human Needs," *Studies in the Spirituality of the Jesuits*, op. cit., pp. 106-7.
5. Marie Edwards and Eleanor Hoover, *The Challenge of Being Single* (New York: New American Library, Signet Books, 1975), pp. 205, 214.

POEM: *Religion*

1. Merrit Malloy, *My Song for Him Who Never Sang to Me* (New York: Crown Publishers, Inc., 1975), p. 77.

CHAPTER NINE: *Woman as Pawn*

1. Version by Thomas MacDonagh, "Eve," *The Faber Book of Irish Verse*, ed. John Montague (London: Faber Paperbacks, 1974), p. 71.
2. Alla Bozarth-Campbell, *Womanpriest* (Paramus, N.J.: Paulist Press, 1978), p. 171.
3. *The Catholic Voice* (Oakland, Calif.), 8 October 1979, p. 6.
4. Barbara Benedict Bunker and Edith Whitfield Seashore, "Power, Collusion, Intimacy-Sexuality Support: Breaking the Sex-Role Stereotypes in Social and Organizational Settings," in *Beyond Sex Roles*, ed. Alice Sargent (St. Paul: West Publishing, 1977), p. 368.
5. Joan Ohanneson, *Women's Gifts: Ministry as Self-Definition, Study Guide to Filmstrip* (Minneapolis: Winston Press, 1979), p. 3.
6. Ibid., p. 3.
7. Dody Donnelly, *Team* (New York: Paulist Press, 1977), p. 68.

CHAPTER TEN: *Women in Church/Women in Society*

1. Patricia Martin Doyle, "Women and Religion: Psychological and Cultural Implications," in *Religion and Sexism*, ed. Rosemary Radford Reuther (New York: Simon & Schuster, 1974), p. 17. See also Paul Tillich, *Systematic Theology*, 3 vols. (Chicago: University of Chicago Press, 1951-1963), 3:293-94.
2. Barbara Brown Zikmund, "Women's Reformation in Motion," *Witness*, May 1978, p. 17.
3. John T. Muthig, "News in Focus," *San Francisco Monitor*, 22 January 1976. See also the original text of the Pastoral Commission of

the Sacred Congregation for the Evangelization of Peoples, "The Participation of Women in World Evangelization," in *Christ to the World* (English edition), vol. 22, no. 1 (1977).

4. *Gaudium et Spes*, No. 4.
5. Raymond E. Brown, *Biblical Reflections on Crises Facing the Church* (New York: Paulist Press, 1975), pp. 48-49.
6. *Gaudium et Spes*, No. 4.
7. "Canonists Await Revised Code Laws," *National Catholic Reporter*, 26 October 1979.
8. Anthony Bevilaqua, *The ERA in Debate/What Can It Mean for Church Law?* (Toledo, Ohio: Canon Law Society of America, 1978), p. 53.
9. Ibid., p. 57.
10. Zikmund, "Women's Reformation in Motion," p. 17.
11. Joan Chittister, *Brotherly Love in Today's Church*, reprinted through courtesy of Editors of America, America Press, Inc., 1977 (Erie, Pa.: Bent Press, 1977), p. 2.
12. M. Nadine Foley, "Women Religious and the Mission of the Church Today" (Address given at the National Assembly of the Leadership Conference of Women Religious, St. Paul, Minn., August 26, 1975). Reprinted in *New Visions/New Roles: Women in the Church* (Washington, D.C.: Leadership Conference of Women Religious of USA, 1975), p. 61.

POEM: *My Name Is Waiting*

1. From a talk given at the Second Conference on the Ordination of Roman Catholic Women, Baltimore, Maryland, November 12, 1978.

CHAPTER ELEVEN: *The Bishop as Healer*

1. Patricia Noone, *Mary for Today* (Chicago: Thomas More Press, 1977), p. 160. See also Adrienne Rich, "When We Dead Awaken" in "Writing as Revision," *College English* 34 (1972): 23.
2. Leo T. Maher (Bishop of San Diego), *Pastoral Letter*, 15 August 1974, p. 4.
3. Ibid., pp. 5, 6.
4. Carrol T. Dozier (Bishop of Memphis), *Pastoral Letter to the People of the Diocese of Memphis*, 6 January 1975, p. 3.
5. Ibid., pp. 2-6.
6. William D. Borders (Archbishop of Baltimore), "Women in the Church: Reflections on Women in the Mission and Ministry of the Church," *Pastoral Letter Addressed to the Priests and People of the Archdiocese of Baltimore*, 19 August 1977, p. 2.
7. Ibid., pp. 2, 8-9.
8. Charles A. Buswell (Bishop of Pueblo), "Ecclesial Affirmative Action: A Matter of Simple Justice," *Catholic Crosswinds* (Pueblo, Colorado), December 1975, p. 1.

9. Ibid., p. 4.
10. Ibid., p. 3.
11. The Roman Catholic Bishops of Minnesota (John D. Roach—Archbishop of St. Paul and Minneapolis; Paul E. Anderson—Bishop of Duluth; Victor H. Balke—Bishop of Crookston; Raymond A. Lucker—Bishop of New Ulm; George H. Speltz—Bishop of St. Cloud; Loras J. Watters—Bishop of Winona; and John F. Kinney—Auxiliary Bishop of St. Paul and Minneapolis), *Woman: Pastoral Reflections* (St. Paul: Minnesota Catholic Conference), 21 March 1979, p. 6.
12. Ibid., pp. 6, 12, 13, 7.
13. Ibid., pp. 8, 9, 11.
14. Elizabeth Schüssler Fiorenza, "Feminist Spirituality, Christian Identity, and Catholic Vision," in *Womanspirit Rising: A Feminist Reader in Religion*, eds. Carol P. Christ and Judith Plaskow (San Francisco: Harper & Row, 1979), p. 147.
15. The Roman Catholic Bishops of Minnesota, *Woman*, p. 20.
16. Maurice J. Dingman (Bishop of Des Moines), "Women and the Church," *Pastoral Bulletin* 11, no. 4 (9 April 1976): 6.
17. P. Francis Murphy (Auxiliary Bishop of Baltimore), "The Future Based on Present/New Experiences" (Public address given in Richmond, Va., October 2, 1977). Printed in *Origins*, 13 October 1977, p. 268.
18. Ibid., p. 271.
19. Ibid., p. 268.
20. Cletus Wessels, "Priests' Liberation" (Address given at Priests for Equality Conference, November 1978). Printed in *Priests for Equality*, July 1979, pp. 1, 4.

CHAPTER TWELVE: *Priests and Women*

1. Federation of Diocesan Liturgical Commissions, "Statement on Women in Liturgical Ministry," *Newsletter* (Supplement), March 1975.
2. Megan McKenna, *Study Guide for Woman: A Many-Media Resource in Human Liberation*, prods. Joan Ohanneson and Mary Littell, A Teleketics Presentation (Los Angeles: Franciscan Communications Center, 1973).
3. Ibid.

CHAPTER THIRTEEN: *Women's Ordination*

1. Pope Paul VI, *On the Development of Peoples*, nos. 15, 16.
2. Pope John XXIII, *Peace on Earth*, no. 15.
3. Fran Ferder, *Called to Break Bread?* (Mt. Rainier, Maryland: Quixote Center, 1978), p. 14.
4. Ibid., pp. 10-11.
5. Ibid., pp. 11-12.

6. "Pope to Hear from Berkeley," *San Francisco Examiner & Chronicle*, 21 March 1977. See reprint of complete text, "Letter to the Apostolic Delegate by Jesuit Theologians on the Faculty of the Jesuit School of Theology in Berkeley, California," in *Origins*, 7 April 1977.
7. Nancy Hardesty and Letha Scanzoni, *All We're Meant to Be* (Waco, Texas: Word Books, 1975), pp. 179, 171.
8. Barbara Brown Zikmund, "Women's Reformation in Motion," *Witness*, May 1978, p. 19.
9. Patricia Noone, *Mary for Today* (Chicago: Thomas More Press, 1977), p. 145.
10. Elizabeth Schüssler Fiorenza, "Feminist Spirituality, Christian Identity, and Catholic Vision," in *Womanspirit Rising: A Feminist Reader in Religion*, eds. Carol P. Christ and Judith Plaskow (San Francisco: Harper & Row, 1979), pp. 144-45.
11. Women's Ordination Conference, Regional Meeting, Denver, Colorado, November 4, 1979.
12. Georgia Fuller, "Catholics for Women's Ordination: Confronting the Roman Patriarchy," *Witness*, May 1978, p. 8.

CHAPTER FOURTEEN: *To Whom Can Women Turn?*

1. The Roman Catholic Bishops of Minnesota, *Woman: Pastoral Reflections* (St. Paul: Minnesota Catholic Conference), 21 March 1979, p. 11.

CHAPTER FIFTEEN: *Women as Prophets*

1. Pope Paul VI, Address to final session of Vatican Commission on Women, January 31, 1976.
2. W. H. Auden, "For the Time Being: A Christmas Oratorio" in *Collected Larger Poems* (New York: Random House, 1969), p. 153.
3. Original Text of Sister Theresa Kane, *Greeting to Pope John Paul II* (Address given in Washington, D.C., October 7, 1979). Reprinted in *Origins*, 18 October 1979, pp. 284-85.
4. Members of Catholic Advocates for Equality, P.O. Box 651, Hyattsville, Maryland 20782.
5. "Statement of the Women Who Stood During John Paul II's Speech at the Immaculate Conception Shrine, Washington, D.C.," (October 7, 1979), *New Women/New Church*, November 1979, p. 8. (Originally published by Catholic Advocates for Equality, including second part entitled "Magnificat for Today.")

CHAPTER SIXTEEN: *Woman as Gift*

1. Rainer Maria Rilke, *Letters to a Young Poet*, trans. by M. D. Herter Norton (W. W. Norton: New York, 1934), p. 65.

2. M. Nadine Foley, "Women Religious and the Mission of the Church Today" (Address given at the National Assembly of the Leadership Conference of Women Religious, St. Paul, Minn., August 26, 1975). Reprinted in *New Visions/New Roles: Women in the Church* (Washington, D. C.: Leadership Conference of Women Religious of USA, 1975), pp. 62-63.
3. Dorothy Donnelly, "And the Almond Tree Blossomed!" *Catholic Charismatic*, February 1977, p. 37.
4. Thomas Roberdeau, "The Secret Cipher" (unpublished poem).
5. Joan Chittister (Address given to Leadership Conference of Women Religious Assembly, Chicago, Illinois, August 28, 1977).
6. Saint Anselm, *Proslogium, Monologium,* trans. Sidney Norton Deane (Chicago: Open Court Publishing, 1903), p. 2. See also Joseph Wilhelm and Thomas B. Scannell, "Introduction," *Manual of Catholic Theology* (New York: Benziger Bros., 1899), p. xxi.
7. "Introduction," *Journeying* (Washington, D.C.: Leadership Conference of Women Religious), July 1977.
8. Joan Ohanneson, *Women's Gifts: Ministry as Self-Definition,* filmstrip with Mary Ann Finch (Minneapolis: Winston Press, 1979).
9. Margaret Ellen Traxler, "Letter to the Editor," *National Catholic Reporter*, 16 May 1975.
10. *Sacrum Commercium,* "Francis and His Lady Poverty," based on Chapter 6, in "The Banquet and Lady Poverty," ed. Marion A. Habig (Chicago: Franciscan Herald Press, 1973), nos. 65, 66, pp. 1594-95.